Learning PyTorch 2.0

Second Edition

Utilize PyTorch 2.3 and CUDA 12 to experiment neural networks and deep learning models

Matthew Rosch

Published by: GitforGits

Publisher: Sonal Dhandre

www.gitforgits.com

support@gitforgits.com

Printed in India

First Printing: October 2024

ISBN: 978-81-19177-91-2

Cover Design by: Kitten Publishing

Prologue

My goal was clear when I first wrote the original edition of Learning PyTorch 2.0: to create a practical, hands-on book that would help developers and engineers harness the power of PyTorch for building neural networks. PyTorch quickly became the go-to choice for researchers and production environments. As the framework evolved, it became evident that there was more to explore and more to learn. I seized the opportunity to work on the second edition, knowing it was the perfect time to expand on the core concepts and bring in the latest advancements from PyTorch 2.3 and CUDA 12.

This edition marks a significant shift in PyTorch's approach to optimization, enhancing both performance and flexibility. The introduction of torch.compile() provides a tool that will significantly boost the training and inference speed of models. This update allows developers to maximize the potential of their neural networks without the need to rewrite them from scratch. From my experience, I can say with confidence that incorporating such powerful optimizations into the core of your development process makes a huge difference when working with real-world data. I made sure this feature, among others, is highlighted throughout the book because it is an important one.

In this second edition, I've continued to use the fish dataset to help you grasp the core concepts of PyTorch. I made sure that the practical programs in this book are not just theoretical. They are tools you can adapt and apply in your own projects. I've always stressed the value of working with real-world data, and I'm confident these examples will equip you with practical skills you can use directly in production environments. I've made sure to include new topics like multi-model serving and versioning when deploying models with TorchServe. This is an essential part of modern machine learning pipelines. As we move toward more complex deployments, you must know how to handle multiple models simultaneously, serve them efficiently, and ensure their versions are properly tracked. This edition will show you how to set up TorchServe for serving models, monitoring performance, and scaling them to meet production needs.

This second edition addresses migration between frameworks in a way that differs from the first. I frequently encounter developers who have spent years building models in TensorFlow but now want to migrate to PyTorch. I have dedicated a chapter to using the ONNX format to move models between TensorFlow and PyTorch seamlessly. I wish I had this when I started making the transition. It will undoubtedly prove extremely useful to those of you who need to bridge the gap between frameworks.

Finally, I want to highlight the expanded coverage of advanced neural network architectures. Today's applications demand more than just the basics. They require us to move beyond image recognition, natural language processing, and other tasks. I've taken a deeper dive into transformer models and how to use these architectures effectively in PyTorch because that's what you need to know. From my experience, I know these models are transforming the industry. I want to make sure my readers can use them confidently.

This second edition has the latest tools, libraries, and features. It's as practical as possible, whether you're building research models or deploying them in production. This edition will help you optimize, deploy, and scale with the latest PyTorch innovations.

Content

Preface

"Learning PyTorch 2.0, Second Edition" is a fast-learning, hands-on book that emphasizes practical PyTorch scripting and efficient model development using PyTorch 2.3 and CUDA 12. This edition is centered on practical applications and presents a concise methodology for attaining proficiency in the most recent features of PyTorch. The book presents a practical program based on the fish dataset which provides step-by-step guidance through the processes of building, training and deploying neural networks, with each example prepared for immediate implementation.

Given your familiarity with machine learning and neural networks, this book offers concise explanations of foundational topics, allowing you to proceed directly to the practical, advanced aspects of PyTorch programming. The key learnings include the design of various types of neural networks, the use of torch.compile() for performance optimization, the deployment of models using TorchServe, and the implementation of quantization for efficient inference. Furthermore, you will also learn to migrate TensorFlow models to PyTorch using the ONNX format.

The book employs essential libraries, including torchvision, torchserve, tf2onnx, onnxruntime, and requests, to facilitate seamless integration of PyTorch with production environments. Regardless of whether the objective is to fine-tune models or to deploy them on a large scale, this second edition is designed to ensure maximum efficiency and speed, with practical PyTorch scripting at the forefront of each chapter.

In this book you will learn:

- Master tensor manipulations and advanced operations using PyTorch's efficient tensor libraries.
- Build feedforward, convolutional, and recurrent neural networks from scratch.
- Implement transformer models for modern natural language processing tasks.
- Use CUDA 12 and mixed precision training (AMP) to accelerate model training and inference.
- Deploy PyTorch models in production using TorchServe, including multi-model serving and versioning.
- Migrate TensorFlow models to PyTorch using ONNX format for seamless cross-framework compatibility.
- Optimize neural network architectures using torch.compile() for improved speed and efficiency.
- Utilize PyTorch's Quantization API to reduce model size and speed up inference.
- Setup custom layers and architectures for neural networks to tackle domain-specific problems.
- Monitor and log model performance in real-time using TorchServe's built-in tools and configurations.

GitforGits

Prerequisites

This book is much more targeted to those who want to deepen their practical knowledge of how to efficiently build, train, and deploy the most common and popular neural network models using Pytorch 2.x and CUDA 12. What it requires of you is simply the fundamentals of machine learning.

Codes Usage

Are you in need of some helpful code examples to assist you in your programming and documentation? Look no further! Our book offers a wealth of supplemental material, including code examples and exercises.

Not only is this book here to aid you in getting your job done, but you have our permission to use the example code in your programs and documentation. However, please note that if you are reproducing a significant portion of the code, we do require you to contact us for permission.

But don't worry, using several chunks of code from this book in your program or answering a question by citing our book and quoting example code does not require permission. But if you do choose to give credit, an attribution typically includes the title, author, publisher, and ISBN. For example, "Learning PyTorch 2.0, Second Edition by Matthew Rosch".

If you are unsure whether your intended use of the code examples falls under fair use or the permissions outlined above, please do not hesitate to reach out to us at support@gitforgits.com.

We are happy to assist and clarify any concerns.

Acknowledgement

I owe a tremendous debt of gratitude to GitforGits, for their unflagging enthusiasm and wise counsel throughout the entire process of writing this book. Their knowledge and careful editing helped make sure the piece was useful for people of all reading levels and comprehension skills. In addition, I'd like to thank everyone involved in the publishing process for their efforts in making this book a reality. Their efforts, from copyediting to advertising, made the project what it is today.

Finally, I'd like to express my gratitude to everyone who has shown me unconditional love and encouragement throughout my life. Their support was crucial to the completion of this book. I appreciate your help with this endeavour and your continued interest in my career.

CHAPTER 1: INTRODUCTION TO PYTORCH 2.3 AND CUDA 12

Overview

To begin with, this chapter is aimed to explore the foundational concepts necessary for building and training neural networks using PyTorch 2.3 and CUDA 12. It starts with revisiting the essentials of neural networks, highlighting how neural networks have evolved to become the backbone of modern AI applications like image recognition, natural language processing, and autonomous systems. You will learn about the structure of neural networks, the role of input, hidden, and output layers, and how weights and biases are adjusted through learning processes such as backpropagation and gradient descent.

As the chapter progresses, you will dive into the evolution of neural networks, discussing how deeper architectures and newer techniques have allowed for more accurate models capable of tackling complex tasks. This section will guide you through the advancements in architecture design, optimization algorithms like Adam, and techniques such as regularization and dropout that improve model generalization. Additionally, you will encounter insights from industry experts on how these developments are shaping modern AI research and production.

You will then move on to PyTorch 2.3, learning how this framework has become a favorite among researchers and developers for its flexibility and powerful dynamic computational graphs. This chapter will introduce you to the latest features of PyTorch 2.3, focusing on how it integrates seamlessly with CUDA 12 to accelerate neural network training on NVIDIA GPUs. The final section will guide you through setting up PyTorch and CUDA 12 on a Linux environment, ensuring you have everything you need to leverage GPU acceleration for faster training and inference.

Essentials of Neural Networks

Evolution of Neural Networks

Over the past decade, neural networks have emerged as the driving force behind some of the most significant advances in AI. From powering virtual assistants to enabling self-driving cars, neural networks have transformed industries and pushed the boundaries of what machines are capable of. The ability of neural networks to learn from data and improve their performance over time has been a key factor in their success, particularly in tasks that require complex decision-making, pattern recognition, and predictions.

A major area where neural networks have made an indelible mark is in **`deep learning`** which is a subset of machine learning that deals with networks that have many layers. These deeper networks can capture intricate patterns in large datasets, something traditional machine learning algorithms struggle to do. For example, in **`image recognition`**, neural networks are capable of identifying objects in pictures with an accuracy that often surpasses human performance. Similarly, in **`natural language processing (NLP)`**, models like OpenAI's **`GPT`** have demonstrated the ability to generate human-like text and perform language translation, question answering, and content summarization.

As neural networks have achieved unprecedented success across multiple domains, research has intensified in exploring new architectures, training methods, and applications. Advances in hardware, such as **Graphics Processing Units (GPUs)** and **Tensor Processing Units (TPUs)**, have played a critical role in enabling the large-scale training of neural networks, which was previously computationally prohibitive.

One of the notable trends in research is the focus on **scaling up neural networks** to larger architectures. For instance, models like **GPT-4** and **PaLM** consist of billions of parameters, trained on vast datasets, making them highly capable of generalizing across multiple tasks. Scaling neural networks to this level allows them to not only solve specific problems but also exhibit a broader understanding of various tasks.

While the success of neural networks is evident, the question arises: what exactly makes these networks so powerful? To answer this, we need to look at the structure and mechanics of a neural network.

Structure of Neural Networks

At the foundation of any neural network lies its structure, which consists of layers of interconnected nodes, often referred to as **neurons**. These neurons are organized into distinct layers that process the input data step by step, transforming it into the final output.

Neural networks are typically made up of three main types of layers:

- **Input Layer**: The input layer is responsible for receiving raw data from the outside world. Each neuron in this layer represents a feature from the dataset, such as the pixels in an image or the words in a sentence.
- **Hidden Layers**: The hidden layers are where the majority of processing takes place. These layers apply transformations to the data, enabling the network to learn complex representations. The term "deep learning" comes from networks that have multiple hidden layers, which allow them to capture more intricate patterns in the data.
- **Output Layer**: Finally, the output layer produces the network's final prediction or decision. The number of neurons in this layer depends on the task—whether it's a binary classification problem, multi-class classification, or regression.

Each neuron in a neural network is connected to neurons in adjacent layers through **weighted connections**. These weights control the strength of the connection between neurons, and they are the primary variables that the network learns during training. Each neuron also has an associated **bias**, which helps the network adjust the activation of neurons, making the model more flexible and capable of capturing complex patterns.

The process of training a neural network involves adjusting these weights and biases so that the model can make accurate predictions. This adjustment is what we refer to as the "learning" process.

How Do Neural Networks Learn?

At the heart of a neural network's learning process is the **adjustment of weights and biases**. When a neural network makes a prediction, it computes an output based on the weighted sum of the inputs it receives from the previous layer. This output is then passed through an **activation function**—a mathematical function that determines whether a neuron should be "activated" or not. Popular activation functions include **ReLU (Rectified Linear Unit)**, **sigmoid**, and **softmax**.

After the network produces an output, the next step is to measure how close or far this prediction is from the actual result. This difference is known as the **error** or **loss**. In order to learn from this error, the network needs to update its weights in such a way that it minimizes this loss in future predictions. This is where **backpropagation** and **gradient descent** come into play.

Backpropagation and Gradient Descent

Backpropagation is the algorithm used to compute the gradients (partial derivatives) of the loss function with respect to each weight in the network. It works by calculating the error at the output layer and then propagating this error backward through the network, layer by layer. This allows the network to determine how each weight contributed to the error.

Once these gradients are computed, the network uses **gradient descent**—an optimization algorithm that adjusts the weights in the direction that reduces the error. Gradient descent iteratively updates the weights so that the network "learns" to make better predictions. There are different variations of gradient descent:

- **Batch Gradient Descent**: Calculates the gradient based on the entire dataset.
- **Stochastic Gradient Descent (SGD)**: Updates the weights based on one data point at a time.
- **Mini-Batch Gradient Descent**: A compromise between the two, where updates are made after processing a small batch of data.

The role of gradient descent is essential, as it allows the network to find the optimal set of weights that minimize the loss function. This process is repeated for multiple iterations, called **epochs**, until the model converges—meaning the loss function reaches a minimum value.

Experts in the field of deep learning have highlighted the efficiency of backpropagation and gradient descent in training deep networks. **Yann LeCun**, a pioneer in deep learning, has referred to backpropagation as "the essence of deep learning," as it allows for efficient learning in deep neural networks, which may consist of millions of parameters. Backpropagation and gradient descent work hand in hand to refine the weights and ensure that the network becomes better at predicting the correct output as it processes more data.

Advanced Techniques in Neural Network Training

While backpropagation and gradient descent form the backbone of neural network training, several advanced techniques have further enhanced the performance of neural networks, particularly in large-scale models.

- **Regularization**: Regularization techniques like **L2 regularization** and **dropout** help prevent overfitting, which occurs when a network performs well on training data but fails to generalize to unseen data. Regularization ensures that the network does not rely too heavily on any particular set of neurons, making it more robust to variations in the data.
- **Learning Rate Schedules**: Adjusting the learning rate over time has proven to be highly effective in improving the performance of neural networks. Techniques like **learning rate decay** and **cyclical learning rates** allow the network to make larger updates initially and smaller adjustments as it converges, leading to more stable training.
- **Optimization Algorithms**: While **SGD** is a simple and widely used optimizer, more advanced algorithms like **Adam** and **RMSProp** have become popular due to their ability to adaptively adjust the learning rate for each parameter. These optimizers help speed up convergence and often lead to better performance on complex tasks.

The evolution of neural networks has given rise to numerous architectures tailored to specific tasks. **Convolutional Neural Networks (CNNs)**, for instance, are widely used for image-related tasks, whereas **Recurrent Neural Networks (RNNs)** and **Long Short-Term Memory (LSTM)** networks are popular in time-series and sequence data.

Moreover, newer architectures such as **transformers** have revolutionized fields like natural language processing by enabling models to handle long-range dependencies in data. These innovations have made it possible to tackle more complex problems and achieve state-of-the-art performance in a variety of domains.

Future of Neural Networks

The future of neural networks looks promising, with ongoing research focusing on making networks more efficient, scalable, and interpretable. Techniques like **neural architecture search (NAS)**, which automates the process of designing neural networks, and **transfer learning**, where models pre-trained on large datasets can be fine-tuned for specific tasks, are paving the way for faster and more effective model development.

In addition, as neural networks grow in scale and complexity, efforts to make them more interpretable are gaining traction. **Explainable AI (XAI)** is a field dedicated to making neural network decisions more transparent, allowing humans to understand why a model made a particular prediction—critical in domains like healthcare and autonomous systems.

Neural networks have come a long way from their initial conception. Their structure, learning process, and the techniques used to train them have evolved significantly, making them a powerful tool in the AI toolkit. As research continues and new advancements emerge, neural networks are poised to solve even more complex challenges, further transforming the landscape of artificial intelligence. In the upcoming chapters, we will delve deeper into PyTorch 2.3 and how it can be leveraged to build and train neural networks. We will also explore how it has been optimized for GPU acceleration, using CUDA 12, significantly speeding up the process of training deep neural networks. In essence, neural networks, by emulating the structure and functionality of the human brain, have revolutionized the field of artificial intelligence. They have opened new avenues for developing intelligent systems capable of performing complex tasks with little to no explicit programming, thus marking the dawn of an exciting era in technology.

Introduction to PyTorch 2.3

Now that we are familiar with the fundamentals of neural networks, we will move on to learn PyTorch, a tool that plays a vital role in the process of developing and training these networks. Among the many tools available to developers and researchers, **PyTorch** stands out as a framework that has significantly shaped the field of AI. It is not only a powerful tool for building and training deep learning models but has also become synonymous with flexibility, efficiency, and accessibility.

Over the past few years, PyTorch has emerged as one of the most popular deep learning frameworks, adopted by industry leaders, research labs, and academic institutions alike. Developed by **Facebook AI Research (FAIR)**, PyTorch has established itself as the go-to framework for deep learning tasks, from research experimentation to large-scale production systems. Its flexibility in model building, dynamic computational graph, and strong support for Python have made it an ideal choice for AI practitioners.

Rise of PyTorch in AI and Deep Learning

The success of PyTorch can be attributed to its **dynamic computation graph** (also known as "define-by-run"), which allows models to be defined and modified at runtime, giving developers an unparalleled level of flexibility. Unlike its predecessor **Torch** or other frameworks like **TensorFlow** (which initially used static graphs), PyTorch's dynamic nature enables developers to experiment with models more freely, making it easier to debug, visualize, and iterate during development.

In the early days, deep learning was primarily a research-driven field, and PyTorch quickly became the tool of choice for researchers. Its simplicity in defining models and its tight integration with **NumPy** (a fundamental Python library for numerical computations) allowed researchers to focus on the intricacies of their models rather than the complexities of the framework. In this way, PyTorch's user-friendly interface played a pivotal role in democratizing deep learning, making it accessible to a broader audience of scientists, engineers, and enthusiasts.

With time, PyTorch has evolved from being primarily a research tool to becoming a fully production-ready framework. Through features like **TorchScript** and **TorchServe**,

PyTorch now supports efficient model deployment, bringing research developments into production environments without sacrificing performance. From small startups to tech giants like **Google**, **Microsoft**, and **Amazon**, PyTorch is now widely used across the industry for tasks ranging from image and speech recognition to natural language processing and autonomous driving.

Moreover, PyTorch's vibrant open-source community has contributed to its rapid growth and widespread adoption. Many cutting-edge models—like **transformers** for NLP or **CNNs** for computer vision—have been implemented in PyTorch, with pre-trained versions readily available for developers to fine-tune and deploy. Its ability to seamlessly integrate with other AI tools and libraries has made PyTorch indispensable in the AI and deep learning landscape.

Latest PyTorch 2.3 and It's Capabilities

With the release of **PyTorch 2.3**, the framework continues to push the boundaries of AI development, offering new features and improvements aimed at enhancing model training, deployment, and production readiness. This latest version builds on PyTorch's core strengths—flexibility, dynamic computation graphs, and strong community support—while introducing cutting-edge capabilities that are essential for modern AI tasks.

The PyTorch 2.3 release is packed with features designed to improve both the research and production phases of AI development. By addressing the needs of researchers experimenting with new models and engineers deploying models at scale, PyTorch 2.3 delivers a comprehensive suite of tools for every stage of the AI lifecycle.

According to the official **PyTorch 2.3 release notes**, some of the key features include improved support for **distributed training**, enhancements in **TorchDynamo** (a system for runtime optimization), expanded **ONNX (Open Neural Network Exchange)** support, and tighter integration with hardware like **NVIDIA GPUs**. Each of these features reflects PyTorch's commitment to improving performance while maintaining flexibility and ease of use.

Below is a detailed overview of some of the most important features introduced in PyTorch 2.3:

TorchDynamo for AI Training Optimizations

One of the most exciting additions in PyTorch 2.3 is TorchDynamo, an innovative tool that dynamically compiles models during runtime, optimizing their execution on-the-fly. TorchDynamo works by transforming the model's computational graph in real-time, applying optimization techniques to reduce execution overhead and enhance performance. This is particularly useful for complex models where runtime optimizations can lead to significant speedups in training and inference.

The goal of TorchDynamo is to provide a flexible system that doesn't require significant code changes to improve performance. By compiling sections of code that are commonly executed, it makes PyTorch models run faster while maintaining the same dynamic nature that PyTorch is known for. As a result, developers can enjoy the best of both worlds: PyTorch's intuitive interface and the performance benefits typically associated with static graph frameworks.

With TorchDynamo, AI developers can fine-tune their models for deployment environments, ensuring that training times are minimized while maximizing the model's accuracy. This addition is especially useful for training large models on extensive datasets, where even small performance gains can translate into significant time savings.

Enhanced Distributed Training Support

Training large-scale models across multiple GPUs or machines has become a standard requirement in AI development. PyTorch 2.3 improves upon its already robust distributed training capabilities by adding new features for handling large-scale data parallelism. The framework now supports Fully Sharded Data Parallel (FSDP), a technique that allows for model sharding across multiple devices, significantly reducing memory overhead.

This feature is particularly useful when dealing with massive models that require more memory than any single GPU can provide. By distributing the model's parameters across multiple GPUs, PyTorch 2.3 enables faster training without compromising accuracy or efficiency. Moreover, FSDP integrates seamlessly with other parallelism techniques, such as torch.distributed and DataParallel, making it easier to scale models for both training and inference.

Another important advancement in distributed training is the introduction of Elasticity Support, which allows training processes to dynamically adjust to the available resources. For instance, if a GPU node fails during training, PyTorch can automatically adjust the training schedule to ensure continuity, preventing training from halting altogether. This feature is critical for deploying models in cloud environments, where resource availability can fluctuate.

ONNX Enhancements

- PyTorch's commitment to supporting **ONNX**, an open standard for machine learning model interoperability, continues with PyTorch 2.3. The latest update improves ONNX export functionality, making it easier for PyTorch models to be converted and deployed in other environments. ONNX support is particularly valuable for deploying PyTorch models on platforms that may not natively support PyTorch, such as mobile or edge devices, or for integrating with other machine learning frameworks.
- With expanded ONNX support, PyTorch 2.3 ensures that AI developers can take full advantage of ONNX's ecosystem, which includes hardware-accelerated runtimes like **ONNX Runtime**. This is crucial for organizations that want to develop models in PyTorch but deploy them across a variety of platforms for production use cases, such as mobile applications, embedded systems, and cloud-based inference services.

TorchServe for Model Deployment

As PyTorch has grown in popularity for model development, there has been a growing demand for tools that facilitate seamless deployment. TorchServe, a model-serving framework developed in collaboration with AWS, addresses this need by offering an easy-to-use, scalable solution for deploying PyTorch models in production environments. TorchServe simplifies the deployment process by offering features such as multi-model serving, version control, and metrics logging, making it ideal for production-scale AI applications.

PyTorch 2.3 builds on TorchServe's capabilities by providing tighter integration with other PyTorch tools, making it easier to move from research to production without major code rewrites. With TorchServe, organizations can confidently deploy their models, knowing they have the support for scaling, monitoring, and managing AI workflows.

Expanded GPU Support

- Given that GPUs are a critical component of training deep learning models, PyTorch 2.3 introduces improved GPU utilization features. PyTorch now fully supports **NVIDIA's Ampere architecture** and **Tensor Cores**, offering enhanced performance for both training and inference. By taking advantage of **mixed precision training**—a technique that uses lower precision (16-bit floating-point) for certain operations—PyTorch 2.3 significantly speeds up training times while maintaining model accuracy.
- Additionally, PyTorch 2.3 offers better support for **Intel GPUs** through **SYCL** integration, making it easier for developers to optimize their models for different hardware environments. This expanded support ensures that PyTorch remains a versatile framework that can be deployed on a wide range of devices, from high-end data centers to consumer-grade hardware.

TorchVision and Other Domain Libraries

- PyTorch 2.3 also brings updates to its domain libraries, including **TorchVision**, **TorchText**, and **TorchAudio**. These libraries are essential for handling specific types of data—images, text, and audio, respectively—and the updates ensure that PyTorch remains a comprehensive solution for building and training models across multiple domains.
- For instance, **TorchVision 0.15** introduces new models, datasets, and transforms to further simplify computer vision tasks. Similarly, **TorchText** and **TorchAudio** have been updated to include new functionality, making it easier to process language and sound data in AI applications.

PyTorch 2.3's feature set clearly demonstrates its ability to bridge the gap between research and production. The combination of **TorchDynamo** for runtime optimization, **distributed training improvements**, **expanded ONNX support**, and **TorchServe** for seamless deployment, all contribute to making PyTorch 2.3 an indispensable tool for modern AI development.

For researchers, PyTorch 2.3 offers unparalleled flexibility in designing and testing new models. Its dynamic computation graph, intuitive API, and robust debugging tools make it a favorite for academic experimentation. For organizations, PyTorch 2.3 ensures that models can be quickly and efficiently deployed into production environments, with tools that support scaling, monitoring, and optimization.

CUDA 12 and Deep Learning

Training neural networks, especially those with large architectures, can be both time-consuming and computationally expensive. This is where **CUDA (Compute Unified Device Architecture)**, developed by **NVIDIA**, plays a transformative role. CUDA is a parallel computing platform and API that enables developers to use NVIDIA GPUs for general-purpose computing, dramatically accelerating the performance of deep learning models.

With the release of **CUDA 12**, NVIDIA continues to push the boundaries of parallel computing. CUDA 12 introduces various optimizations and enhancements that make it an essential tool for AI researchers and developers. One of the key features of CUDA 12 is its ability to leverage the parallelism inherent in GPU architecture. Unlike central processing units (CPUs), which are optimized for serial processing tasks, GPUs are designed with thousands of cores capable of executing thousands of threads simultaneously. This many-core architecture makes GPUs uniquely suited for the highly parallelizable computations required in deep learning.

Accelerated Deep Learning using CUDA

At the heart of deep learning are operations such as **matrix multiplications**, **convolutions**, and **tensor manipulations**. These operations are inherently parallelizable, meaning that they can be divided into smaller tasks that can be processed simultaneously. For instance, in the case of matrix multiplication—one of the most computationally intensive operations in neural networks—the elements of the resulting matrix can be computed independently of each other. CUDA 12 allows these operations to be distributed across thousands of GPU cores, significantly speeding up the process.

With each new version of CUDA, NVIDIA improves the efficiency of this parallelism. CUDA 12 includes optimizations for **mixed precision training**, a technique that accelerates deep learning by using 16-bit floating-point precision (FP16) instead of the standard 32-bit (FP32) for certain operations. Mixed precision reduces memory usage and allows for faster computations without sacrificing model accuracy. Coupled with **Tensor Cores**—specialized hardware introduced in NVIDIA GPUs—CUDA 12 can deliver up to several times the performance of previous generations when handling these operations.

CUDA 12 also includes **multi-streaming support**, enabling GPUs to execute multiple independent tasks concurrently. This is especially useful in deep learning when training models on large datasets, as it allows data preprocessing, model computation, and gradient updates to occur in parallel. These optimizations help reduce the time required to train large models, making it possible to iterate faster and explore more complex architectures.

Blend of CUDA and PyTorch

While CUDA 12 offers powerful hardware capabilities, its true potential is realized when paired with software frameworks that can fully leverage its features. **PyTorch**, with its dynamic computation graph and intuitive design, has emerged as one of the most popular frameworks for deep learning. The combination of CUDA's hardware acceleration and PyTorch's flexibility forms a powerful toolchain for AI and deep learning development.

One of the standout features of PyTorch is its seamless integration with CUDA. With a simple modification in the code, developers can transfer their computations from the CPU to the GPU, allowing PyTorch to take full advantage of CUDA's parallel processing capabilities. PyTorch's core data structure, the **tensor**, has built-in support for CUDA, making it easy to move tensors between the CPU and GPU. By calling **.cuda()** on a tensor or model, developers can harness the power of CUDA without rewriting their code from scratch.

This integration has made PyTorch the framework of choice for both researchers and industry practitioners. Researchers benefit from the ease of experimentation with PyTorch's dynamic computation graph, while engineers in industry can take advantage of CUDA's GPU acceleration to scale models in production environments. This blend of hardware and software enables the development of large-scale AI systems, such as natural language processing models, recommendation systems, and image classification networks.

Expert Insights on CUDA and PyTorch

Leading AI researchers and engineers have consistently highlighted the significance of the combination of CUDA and PyTorch for the advancement of deep learning. **Ian Goodfellow**, one of the pioneers of **Generative Adversarial Networks (GANs)**, has emphasized the role of GPUs and CUDA in making the training of large networks feasible. He stated that "the parallelism enabled by GPUs, combined with frameworks like PyTorch, has been critical in bringing deep learning from academic labs to practical applications in industry."

Similarly, **Soumith Chintala**, a core contributor to PyTorch, has pointed out the importance of CUDA integration in PyTorch's rapid adoption by the AI community. In a recent talk, Chintala remarked, "PyTorch was designed with ease of use and flexibility in mind, but its true power comes from being able to seamlessly integrate with CUDA, allowing researchers to develop on a single GPU and scale their work to multiple GPUs without significant code changes."

The significance of CUDA and PyTorch extends beyond research labs. Companies like **Tesla**, **Google**, and **Microsoft** rely on PyTorch and CUDA to train the AI models that power their autonomous vehicles, recommendation systems, and cloud services. For instance, **Tesla** uses PyTorch and CUDA to train its computer vision models, which are deployed in the company's self-driving cars. The ability to train models efficiently on large datasets and then deploy them in production is a critical factor in their success.

Another notable perspective comes from **Andrew Ng**, a leading figure in AI education and research. Ng has emphasized the importance of hardware acceleration in democratizing AI. "Tools like CUDA and frameworks like PyTorch have made it possible for more people to participate in AI development. By reducing the time and resources needed to train models, these tools have significantly lowered the barrier to entry for aspiring AI practitioners."

CUDA for AI Production

The combination of CUDA and PyTorch is not only essential for accelerating deep learning during the research and experimentation phases, but also for scaling AI models to production. With the increasing demand for real-time AI applications—such as voice recognition, fraud detection, and autonomous systems—efficient model training and deployment have become critical.

The ability to train models on **`multi-GPU systems`** using PyTorch's **`DataParallel`** or **`DistributedDataParallel`** modules, while leveraging CUDA's memory optimization and parallel computation, allows AI models to be trained on massive datasets in hours rather than weeks. This is especially important for companies deploying AI models in cloud environments, where the speed of training and inference can directly impact service delivery and cost.

Moreover, CUDA's integration with PyTorch ensures that models trained in research environments can be seamlessly transitioned into production with minimal modifications. **`TorchServe`**, a model-serving framework within the PyTorch ecosystem, allows developers to deploy models trained with CUDA-accelerated PyTorch, ensuring that the performance gains from GPU training are retained during inference. This makes PyTorch not only a research-friendly framework but also a production-ready solution for large-scale AI applications.

The blend of **`CUDA 12`** and **`PyTorch`** represents one of the most powerful combinations in modern AI development. CUDA's ability to accelerate deep learning through parallelism and GPU optimization, coupled with PyTorch's dynamic and flexible framework, has enabled researchers and engineers to push the boundaries of AI.

Setting up PyTorch 2.3 and CUDA 12

With an understanding of how PyTorch and CUDA work together to accelerate deep learning, the next step is to get your environment set up for efficient development. So to begin with, we will walk through the practical steps to install **`CUDA 12`** and **`PyTorch 2.3`** on our Linux **`Ubuntu`**. This setup is essential for leveraging the parallelism and GPU acceleration provided by CUDA to rnable deep learning models getting trained faster and can handle larger datasets.

Installing CUDA 12

Before installing CUDA 12, ensure that our system meets the following requirements:

- Ubuntu 20.04 or 22.04 LTS

- A **NVIDIA GPU** with Compute Capability 5.0 or higher (you can check your GPU's capability at https://developer.nvidia.com/cuda-gpus)
- NVIDIA driver version 520.61.05 or newer

To check your current GPU and driver version, run the following command:

```
nvidia-smi
```

This will display information about your GPU, including the driver version. If your driver is outdated, update it before proceeding.

Add NVIDIA Package Repositories

NVIDIA maintains a package repository that simplifies the installation of CUDA on Ubuntu. To add this repository to your system, follow these steps:

- First, download the NVIDIA repository package:

```
sudo apt-key adv --fetch-keys
https://developer.download.nvidia.com/compute/cuda/repos/
ubuntu$(lsb_release -sr | cut -d. -
f1)/x86_64/7fa2af80.pub
```

- Then, add the CUDA repository to your system:

```
sudo add-apt-repository "deb
https://developer.download.nvidia.com/compute/cuda/repos/
ubuntu$(lsb_release -sr | cut -d. -f1)/x86_64/ /"
```

Install CUDA 12 Toolkit

Once the repository has been added, update your package list and install the CUDA 12 toolkit:

```
sudo apt-get update

sudo apt-get install cuda-12-0
```

This command will install the **`CUDA 12`** toolkit, along with the necessary development libraries.

Set Environment Variables

To ensure that your system can use CUDA 12, you need to update your environment variables.

- Add the following lines to your **.bashrc** file:

```
export PATH=/usr/local/cuda-12.0/bin${PATH:+:${PATH}}

export LD_LIBRARY_PATH=/usr/local/cuda-
12.0/lib64${LD_LIBRARY_PATH:+:${LD_LIBRARY_PATH}}
```

- After editing the file, run the following command to refresh your environment:

```
source ~/.bashrc
```

Verify CUDA Installation

To verify that CUDA 12 has been installed successfully, you can use the **nvcc** command, which is the NVIDIA CUDA Compiler:

```
nvcc --version
```

You should see output indicating that **CUDA 12** is installed and ready to use.

Installing PyTorch 2.3

With CUDA 12 installed, you are now ready to install **PyTorch 2.3**, which will automatically detect CUDA for GPU acceleration.

Using 'pip'

The easiest and most flexible way to install PyTorch is through the Python package manager **pip**. PyTorch provides a convenient command generator on its website, but here are the steps to install it manually.

First, make sure your **pip** version is up to date:

```
pip install --upgrade pip
```

Next, install PyTorch 2.3 with CUDA 12 support by running the following command:

```
pip install torch torchvision torchaudio --index-url
https://download.pytorch.org/whl/cu120
```

This command installs the core **`PyTorch library (torch)`**, **`TorchVision`** for handling computer vision tasks, and **`TorchAudio`** for audio-related tasks, all with **`CUDA 12`** support.

Via Anaconda

Alternatively, if you are using **`Anaconda`** for managing your Python environments, you can install PyTorch using **`conda`**. First, ensure that Anaconda is installed and activated:

```
conda activate
```

Then, run the following command to install PyTorch 2.3 with CUDA 12 support:

```
conda install pytorch torchvision torchaudio pytorch-
cuda=12.0 -c pytorch -c nvidia
```

This command will install PyTorch and the CUDA toolkit using the NVIDIA channel, which ensures compatibility between PyTorch and CUDA.

Verifying PyTorch and CUDA Installation

Once PyTorch and CUDA are installed, it's important to verify that they are working together correctly.

Checking CUDA Availability in PyTorch

Open a Python shell or Jupyter notebook and run the following code to check if PyTorch can detect the CUDA-enabled GPU:

```
import torch

print(torch.cuda.is_available())
```

If PyTorch has been set up correctly with CUDA 12, the output should be **`True`**, indicating that PyTorch can utilize your GPU for computations.

Checking PyTorch and CUDA Versions

To check the installed versions of PyTorch and CUDA, you can also run the following command in your Python environment:

```
print(torch.__version__)  # Should return PyTorch version
(e.g., '2.3.0')

print(torch.version.cuda)  # Should return '12.0' if CUDA
12 is installed
```

This output confirms that PyTorch 2.3 is installed and using CUDA 12 for GPU acceleration.

Installing Jupyter Notebooks

If you are planning to work with Jupyter Notebooks, which are commonly used for experimenting with deep learning models, you can install **Jupyter** using pip:

```
pip install jupyter
```

Once installed, you can launch Jupyter Notebook using the following command:

```
jupyter notebook
```

Now, to ensure that your setup is working correctly, you can run a simple script that performs a tensor operation on the GPU. Open a Python shell or Jupyter notebook and execute the following code:

```
import torch

# Create a tensor and move it to the GPU

x = torch.rand(5, 3)

x = x.cuda()


# Perform a matrix multiplication on the GPU

y = torch.rand(3, 3).cuda()
```

```
result = torch.matmul(x, y)


print(result)

print("Tensor is on GPU:", result.is_cuda)
```

This script generates random tensors, moves them to the GPU, and performs a matrix multiplication using CUDA 12. If your installation is successful, you should see output indicating that the tensor operations are being performed on the GPU.

Summary

With these, you have gained a solid understanding of the fundamentals of neural networks and their evolution over time. You have revisited the structure of neural networks, including the roles of input, hidden, and output layers, and how neurons, weights, and biases work together during the learning process. Concepts like backpropagation and gradient descent, which are essential for training neural networks, were explored in detail, giving you a clear understanding of how these techniques help optimize model performance.

You have also learned about the recent advancements in neural network architectures, such as deep networks, optimization algorithms like Adam, and techniques like regularization and dropout. These advancements are critical for building more accurate and robust models capable of tackling complex tasks in AI and machine learning. Additionally, you were introduced to PyTorch 2.3, where you discovered how its dynamic computation graph and flexible design have made it a favorite among AI researchers and developers. You explored the key features of PyTorch 2.3 and how they enhance both research and production workflows. The integration of PyTorch with CUDA 12 was discussed, allowing you to understand how GPU acceleration can significantly speed up the training of neural networks.

Finally, you successfully set up PyTorch 2.3 and CUDA 12 in a Linux environment, gaining practical skills in configuring your development setup for GPU-accelerated deep learning tasks. These foundational skills prepare you to work efficiently with PyTorch in the upcoming chapters as you dive deeper into building, training, and deploying neural networks.

Chapter 2: Getting Started with Tensors

Overview

In this chapter, you will be introduced to tensors, which serve as the backbone for data representation in PyTorch and deep learning. You will learn about the structure and dimensionality of tensors, including their rank, shape, and size, and how they are used to represent complex datasets. We will also explore various types of tensors, such as empty, zero, ones, and random tensors, and how to create and manipulate them using PyTorch.

As you progress, you'll delve into key tensor terminologies and concepts like scalars, vectors, and matrices, understanding how each is represented in PyTorch and their role in neural networks. The chapter then moves on to practical operations on tensors, covering standard arithmetic operations like addition, subtraction, multiplication, and division, as well as tensor manipulation techniques such as reshaping, slicing, and joining tensors.

Finally, this chapter will introduce advanced tensor operations like broadcasting, matrix multiplication, and aggregation, helping you build a strong foundation for working with tensors in real-world deep learning tasks. By applying these concepts to a real-world dataset, you will gain hands-on experience performing tensor computations, which are essential for building and training neural networks in PyTorch.

Exploring Tensors

A tensor, in the context of deep learning, is a generalization of vectors and matrices to potentially higher dimensions, and is a fundamental data structure in PyTorch. Tensors are a type of data structure used in linear algebra, and like vectors and matrices, you can calculate arithmetic operations with tensors.

Tensors Dimensionality and Types

Tensors are a core unit of data in PyTorch and are represented as multi-dimensional arrays. The dimensionality of a tensor can be described with rank, shape, and size.

- Rank: This simply tells us the number of dimensions in a tensor. A scalar has rank 0, a vector has rank 1, a matrix has rank 2, and a tensor has rank 3 or more.
- Shape: The shape of a tensor is the number of elements in each dimension.
- Size: The total number of items in the tensor, which can be computed as a product of the elements of the shape.

In PyTorch, tensors allow for operations to be performed on GPUs, which can significantly accelerate the computations. They are similar to NumPy's ndarrays, with the addition being that Tensors can also be used on a GPU to accelerate computing.

PyTorch provides various functions to create different types of tensors. Below are a few examples:

- Empty Tensor: torch.empty(size): Returns a tensor of given size filled with uninitialized data. Here, size is a tuple defining the dimension of the tensor.
- Zero Tensor: torch.zeros(size): Returns a tensor filled with zeroes.
- Ones Tensor: torch.ones(size): Returns a tensor filled with ones.
- Random Tensor: torch.rand(size): Returns a tensor filled with random numbers from a uniform distribution in the range [0, 1).

Tensor Concepts and Terminologies

Tensors, the multi-dimensional generalization of scalars, vectors, and matrices, are key to the functionality of PyTorch, a popular deep learning framework. Mastering the concepts associated with tensors is a vital step in harnessing the full power of PyTorch, as these data structures are pivotal for efficiently carrying out computations in deep learning.

Scalar

A scalar is the simplest type of tensor, containing only a single element with no dimensions. When translated into the PyTorch framework, a scalar can be represented as torch.tensor(5). This is a tensor with zero dimensions, a concept that's akin to a point in the realm of geometry – having a position, but lacking extent.

Vector

A vector, on the other hand, is a one-dimensional tensor, similar to a line in geometry. An example of a vector in PyTorch would be torch.tensor([1, 2, 3, 4]). This tensor has a single axis and therefore has an extent or length, with each element corresponding to a point along that axis.

Matrix

Advancing in complexity, a matrix is a two-dimensional tensor, possessing both rows and columns. In PyTorch, it could be represented as torch.tensor([[1, 2], [3, 4]]). Matrices can be thought of as a table of numbers or a grid that spans two directions or axes.

Tensor Operations

An essential aspect of tensor manipulation is the numerous tensor operations supported by PyTorch. These operations cover a broad spectrum, ranging from basic arithmetic operations like addition, subtraction, multiplication, and division to more complex linear algebra functions. Element-wise operations, reduction operations, and comparison operations form a rich palette of tools that make PyTorch an effective and versatile platform for deep learning tasks.

Broadcasting

An especially powerful mechanism of PyTorch is broadcasting, a functionality that allows the framework to deal with arrays of different shapes during arithmetic operations. It extends smaller arrays to match larger ones, allowing element-wise operations to be conducted smoothly, a feature that significantly enhances the flexibility and convenience of array manipulations.

Device

Finally, the 'Device' aspect of PyTorch ensures that tensors can be seamlessly moved to any device memory using the .to method. For example, tensor.to("cuda") facilitates the transfer of the tensor to the GPU, thus enabling hardware-accelerated computations, which are crucial in handling the massive computational demands of deep learning.

All this fundamental understanding sets the stage for more advanced concepts and techniques in deep learning that we will explore in subsequent chapters, starting with a sample program on creating tensors in the next topic.

Sample Program: Creating Tensors

We will dive into creating tensors using PyTorch. We will see how to create an empty tensor, tensors filled with ones, zeros, and random values. To begin with, firstly, we will import the PyTorch library:

```
import torch
```

- Creating an Empty Tensor:

```
empty_tensor = torch.empty(3, 2)

print(empty_tensor)
```

This will create a tensor of shape 3x2 filled with uninitialized data. The output will be something like:

```
tensor([[2.1019e-44, 0.0000e+00],

    [      nan, 0.0000e+00],

    [1.3733e-14, 6.4069e+02]])
```

- Creating a Tensor Filled with Zeros:

```
zero_tensor = torch.zeros(3, 2)
```

```
print(zero_tensor)
```

This will create a tensor of shape 3x2 filled with zeros. The output will be:

```
tensor([[0., 0.],
        [0., 0.],
        [0., 0.]])
```

- Creating a Tensor Filled with Ones:

```
ones_tensor = torch.ones(3, 2)
print(ones_tensor)
```

This will create a tensor of shape 3x2 filled with ones. The output will be:

```
tensor([[1., 1.],
        [1., 1.],
        [1., 1.]])
```

- Creating a Random Tensor:

```
random_tensor = torch.rand(3, 2)
print(random_tensor)
```

This will create a tensor of shape 3x2 filled with random numbers from a uniform distribution on the interval [0, 1). The output will be something like:

```
tensor([[0.6022, 0.9622],
        [0.7817, 0.5994],
        [0.6712, 0.4674]])
```

These basic tensor operations form the building blocks for creating more complex data structures in PyTorch, which is instrumental when modeling neural networks and developing deep learning

applications.

Tensor Data Types

Tensors in Pytorch, have associated data types similar to data types in Python. This data type defines the kind of elements that are contained within the tensor and the possible range of their values.

Below are some of the most commonly used data types:

- **torch.float32** or **torch.float**: 32-bit floating point
- **torch.float64** or **torch.double**: 64-bit, double-precision floating-point
- **torch.float16** or **torch.half**: 16-bit, half-precision floating-point
- **torch.int32** or **torch.int**: 32-bit integer (signed)
- **torch.int64** or **torch.long**: 64-bit integer (signed)
- **torch.bool**: Boolean type

The default data type for tensors is 32-bit floating point. You can change the data type of a tensor using the .to() method as shown below:

```
# Create tensor with default data type (float32)

tensor = torch.ones(3, 2)

print(tensor)

print("Data Type: ", tensor.dtype)


# Changing tensor data type to float64

tensor = tensor.to(torch.float64)

print("\nAfter Changing Data Type to float64:")

print(tensor)

print("Data Type: ", tensor.dtype)
```

```
# Changing tensor data type to int32
tensor = tensor.to(torch.int32)
print("\nAfter Changing Data Type to int32:")
print(tensor)
print("Data Type: ", tensor.dtype)

# Changing tensor data type to boolean
tensor = tensor.to(torch.bool)
print("\nAfter Changing Data Type to boolean:")
print(tensor)
print("Data Type: ", tensor.dtype)
```

The output will be:

```
tensor([[1., 1.],
     [1., 1.],
     [1., 1.]])
Data Type:  torch.float32

After Changing Data Type to float64:

tensor([[1., 1.],
```

```
     [1., 1.],
     [1., 1.]], dtype=torch.float64)
Data Type:  torch.float64


After Changing Data Type to int32:


tensor([[1, 1],
     [1, 1],
     [1, 1]], dtype=torch.int32)
Data Type:  torch.int32


After Changing Data Type to boolean:


tensor([[True, True],
     [True, True],
     [True, True]])
Data Type:  torch.bool
```

It's also worth mentioning that PyTorch provides a function to create a tensor of a specific type, for example: torch.zeros(3,2,dtype=torch.int32). It's also crucial to ensure tensors used in calculations are of the same type, as PyTorch does not perform implicit type conversion.

Standard Arithmetic Operations

We will see how to perform basic arithmetic operations on tensors. We will cover addition, subtraction, multiplication, and division operations.

Firstly, we will create two tensors of the same shape:

```
# Create two tensors
tensor1 = torch.tensor([1, 2, 3, 4], dtype=torch.float32)
tensor2 = torch.tensor([5, 6, 7, 8], dtype=torch.float32)

print("Tensor 1:", tensor1)
print("Tensor 2:", tensor2)
```

Below is the output:

```
Tensor 1: tensor([1., 2., 3., 4.])
Tensor 2: tensor([5., 6., 7., 8.])
```

- Addition

```
# Addition
result = tensor1 + tensor2
print("Addition Result: ", result)
```

Below is the output:

```
Addition Result:  tensor([ 6.,  8., 10., 12.])
```

- Subtraction

```
# Subtraction
result = tensor1 - tensor2
print("Subtraction Result: ", result)
```

Below is the output:

```
Subtraction Result:  tensor([-4., -4., -4., -4.])
```

- Multiplication

```
# Multiplication (Element-wise)

result = tensor1 * tensor2

print("Multiplication Result: ", result)
```

Below is the output:

```
Multiplication Result:  tensor([ 5., 12., 21., 32.])
```

- Division

```
# Division

result = tensor1 / tensor2

print("Division Result: ", result)
```

Below is the output:

```
Division Result:  tensor([0.2000, 0.3333, 0.4286,
0.5000])
```

Please be informed that the operations are element-wise, meaning they are applied on corresponding elements of the two tensors.

Next, we will get into more complex operations and explore how these basic operations can be combined to implement more complex computations.

Tensor Manipulation

Tensor manipulation in PyTorch typically involves operations like reshaping, slicing, and joining tensors. We will delve into each of these topics.

Reshaping Tensors

Reshaping tensors is a common operation, which allows us to restructure our data to have different numbers of dimensions or different sizes for each dimension.

We will create another tensor and then reshape it:

```
# Create a tensor

tensor = torch.arange(9)

print("Original Tensor:")

print(tensor)


# Reshape the tensor

reshaped_tensor = tensor.view(3, 3)

print("\nReshaped Tensor:")

print(reshaped_tensor)
```

Below is the output:

```
Original Tensor:

tensor([0, 1, 2, 3, 4, 5, 6, 7, 8])


Reshaped Tensor:

tensor([[0, 1, 2],

     [3, 4, 5],

     [6, 7, 8]])
```

Slicing Tensors

Slicing allows us to extract a portion of the tensor. The slicing syntax in PyTorch is quite similar to that in Python and NumPy.

```
# Slicing the tensor

sliced_tensor = reshaped_tensor[0:2, 0:2]

print("\nSliced Tensor:")

print(sliced_tensor)
```

Below is the output:

```
Sliced Tensor:

tensor([[0, 1],

        [3, 4]])
```

Joining Tensors

PyTorch provides several methods to combine tensors, such as torch.cat() and torch.stack(). We will use torch.cat() to concatenate two tensors along a given dimension:

```
# Create two tensors

tensor1 = torch.tensor([1, 2, 3])

tensor2 = torch.tensor([4, 5, 6])


# Concatenate the tensors along dimension 0

concatenated_tensor = torch.cat((tensor1, tensor2))

print("\nConcatenated Tensor:")

print(concatenated_tensor)
```

Below is the output:

```
Concatenated Tensor:

tensor([1, 2, 3, 4, 5, 6])
```

For tensor manipulation, these operations are extremely useful. With a working knowledge of these concepts, you will be able to work effectively with tensors and prepare your data for deep learning models.

Matrix Multiplication

You can perform matrix multiplication using the torch.matmul() function or the @ operator. Both of these methods check the dimensionality of the tensors and apply the appropriate multiplication operation (element-wise multiplication for 1D tensors, matrix multiplication for 2D tensors, batched matrix multiplication for 3D tensors).

We will create two matrices and perform a matrix multiplication operation.

```
# Create two 2D tensors (matrices)

matrix1 = torch.tensor([[1, 2], [3, 4]])

matrix2 = torch.tensor([[5, 6], [7, 8]])


print("Matrix 1:")

print(matrix1)


print("\nMatrix 2:")

print(matrix2)


# Matrix multiplication using torch.matmul()

result = torch.matmul(matrix1, matrix2)

print("\nMatrix Multiplication Result using
```

```
torch.matmul():")
print(result)

# Matrix multiplication using @ operator
result = matrix1 @ matrix2
print("\nMatrix Multiplication Result using @ operator:")
print(result)
```

Below is the output:

```
Matrix 1:
tensor([[1, 2],
     [3, 4]])

Matrix 2:
tensor([[5, 6],
     [7, 8]])

Matrix Multiplication Result using torch.matmul():
tensor([[19, 22],
     [43, 50]])

Matrix Multiplication Result using @ operator:
```

```
tensor([[19, 22],
        [43, 50]])
```

The result of the multiplication operation is calculated by the dot product of rows from the first matrix and columns from the second matrix. This operation is frequently used in deep learning, for instance, when propagating inputs through the layers of a neural network. When multiplying matrices, it is important to keep in mind that the number of rows in the second matrix must be equal to the number of columns in the first matrix.

Manage Tensor Shape Errors

The dealings with tensor shape errors often requires understanding the nature of the operation you are performing and the dimensionality of your tensors. Below are a few common cases where you might encounter shape errors:

Matrix Multiplication

If you are doing matrix multiplication, the number of columns in the first matrix must equal the number of rows in the second matrix. If this condition is not satisfied, you will encounter a size mismatch error.

For example:

```
matrix1 = torch.rand(2, 3)

matrix2 = torch.rand(2, 3)

result = torch.matmul(matrix1, matrix2)  # This will
raise a size mismatch error
```

In the above example, reshaping or transposing matrix2 will resolve the issue:

```
matrix2 = matrix2.t()  # Transpose the matrix

result = torch.matmul(matrix1, matrix2)  # This will not
raise an error
```

Element-wise Operations

If you are doing element-wise operations (like addition, subtraction, etc.), the tensors involved should have the same shape. PyTorch does support broadcasting (a concept borrowed from NumPy), which allows for binary operations on tensors of different sizes, but there are rules to this as well.

For example:

```
tensor1 = torch.rand(2, 3)

tensor2 = torch.rand(2, 2)

result = tensor1 + tensor2  # This will raise a size
mismatch error
```

In the above case, ensuring both tensors have the same shape will fix the error.

Reshaping Tensors

If you are reshaping a tensor, the total number of elements before and after the reshape operation should remain the same. If this isn't the case, you will encounter an error.

For example:

```
tensor = torch.rand(2, 3)

reshaped_tensor = tensor.view(2, 4)  # This will raise an
error
```

In the above case, ensuring the new shape is compatible with the number of elements in the tensor will solve the problem.

Whenever you encounter a shape error, carefully examine the dimensions of the tensors you are working with and the requirements of the operations you are performing. Use methods like .size() or .shape to inspect the size of your tensors and view(), reshape(), or transpose() to manipulate the shape of your tensors when needed.

Aggregation Operations

Aggregation operations are those that reduce the number of elements contained within a tensor. These include operations like finding the sum, mean, maximum, or minimum of the elements.

We will again create a new tensor and perform various aggregation operations:

```
import torch
```

```
# Create a tensor

tensor = torch.tensor([[1, 2, 3], [4, 5, 6]],
dtype=torch.float32)

print("Tensor:")

print(tensor)
```

Below is the output:

```
Tensor:

tensor([[1., 2., 3.],

        [4., 5., 6.]])
```

Sum

Find the sum of all elements in the tensor:

```
# Sum of tensor

sum_val = torch.sum(tensor)

print("\nSum of Tensor Elements: ", sum_val)
```

Below is the output:

```
Sum of Tensor Elements:  tensor(21.)
```

Mean

Compute the mean of the tensor elements:

```
# Mean of tensor

mean_val = torch.mean(tensor)
```

```
print("\nMean of Tensor Elements: ", mean_val)
```

Below is the output:

```
Mean of Tensor Elements:  tensor(3.5)
```

Max

Find the maximum value in the tensor:

```
# Max of tensor

max_val = torch.max(tensor)

print("\nMax of Tensor Elements: ", max_val)
```

Below is the output:

```
Max of Tensor Elements:  tensor(6.)
```

Min

Find the minimum value in the tensor:

```
# Min of tensor

min_val = torch.min(tensor)

print("\nMin of Tensor Elements: ", min_val)
```

Below is the output:

```
Min of Tensor Elements:  tensor(1.)
```

For tasks like normalization, finding the maximum predicted value, and more, these operations are commonly used in machine learning. Remember that the torch.mean() function can only be performed on tensors that use floats. If the data in your tensor is of the integer type, you must first convert it to the float type.

Sample Program: Tensor Manipulations on Fish Dataset

We will now practice all the so far learned tensor manipulations on the **Fish Dataset** available at the following URL:

https://raw.githubusercontent.com/kittenpub/database-repository/main/Fish_Dataset_Pytorch.csv

We will download and load this dataset using **PyTorch** utilities, then perform several common tensor operations, such as reshaping, slicing, aggregation, and broadcasting.

Dataset Loading and Tensor Conversion

First, we will load the Fish Dataset from the above URL. Since this dataset is in CSV format, we can use **Pandas** to load and preprocess it before converting it to a PyTorch tensor.

```
import pandas as pd

# Load the dataset from the URL

url =
"https://raw.githubusercontent.com/kittenpub/database-
repository/main/Fish_Dataset_Pytorch.csv"

fish_data = pd.read_csv(url)


# Preview the first few rows of the dataset

print(fish_data.head())


# Convert the dataset to a tensor, excluding the label
column (assuming the last column is the label)

fish_tensor = torch.tensor(fish_data.iloc[:, :-1].values,
dtype=torch.float32)
```

```
# Show the shape of the tensor

print(f"Shape of the fish tensor: {fish_tensor.shape}")
```

This will load the **`Fish Dataset`** and convert it into a PyTorch tensor, where the data type is **`float32`**. We will exclude the label column (which might represent species or class) and only convert the feature columns into a tensor.

Reshaping the Tensor

Once the data is in tensor format, we may need to reshape the data into different batch sizes for deep learning applications.

```
# Reshaping the tensor

reshaped_tensor = fish_tensor.view(-1, 2)  # Reshape into
2 columns with inferred rows

print(f"Reshaped Tensor (2 columns):
{reshaped_tensor.shape}")


reshaped_tensor_batch = fish_tensor.view(10, -1)  #
Reshape into 10 rows with inferred columns

print(f"Reshaped Tensor (10 rows):
{reshaped_tensor_batch.shape}")
```

In this example, the **`view()`** function is used to reshape the tensor:

- **Reshaped into 2 columns**, where the number of rows is inferred.
- **Reshaped into 10 rows**, where the number of columns is inferred.

Slicing Tensor

We will now perform tensor slicing in order to extract specific rows, columns, or subsections of the data.

```
# Slicing the first 5 rows and the first 3 columns

sliced_tensor = fish_tensor[:5, :3]

print(f"Sliced Tensor (First 5 rows, First 3
columns):\n{sliced_tensor}")
```

Here, we slice the first 5 rows and the first 3 columns of the dataset. This operation is useful for selecting specific parts of the data for analysis or training.

Aggregation Operations

Next, we perform aggregation operations on the Fish Dataset.

```
# Calculate the mean and sum of the dataset along the
rows and columns

mean_tensor = torch.mean(fish_tensor, dim=0)  # Mean
across each column

sum_tensor = torch.sum(fish_tensor, dim=1)    # Sum
across each row



print(f"Mean Tensor (Column-wise): {mean_tensor}")

print(f"Sum Tensor (Row-wise): {sum_tensor}")
```

Here:

- **Column-wise mean**: We calculate the mean of each column.
- **Row-wise sum**: We calculate the sum of values across each row.

Broadcasting Operations

We then can perform broadcasting to automatically expand the dimensions of tensors to make them compatible for element-wise operations. See below:

```
# Perform broadcasting to add a scalar value to all
elements in the tensor

scalar = torch.tensor(10.0)

broadcasted_tensor = fish_tensor + scalar


print(f"Broadcasted Tensor (Added Scalar 10 to All
Elements):\n{broadcasted_tensor}")
```

Here, we add a scalar value (10.0) to each element in the tensor using broadcasting. This operation is performed efficiently without needing to manually reshape the tensor.

Normalization of Data

Next, we perform normalization in order to have the data scaled with a mean of 0 and a standard deviation of 1. This can be done easily with PyTorch operations.

```
# Normalize the tensor (mean = 0, std = 1)

mean = fish_tensor.mean(dim=0, keepdim=True)

std = fish_tensor.std(dim=0, keepdim=True)

normalized_tensor = (fish_tensor - mean) / std


print(f"Normalized Tensor:\n{normalized_tensor}")
```

In this example, we subtract the mean and divide by the standard deviation for each column to normalize the data.

Just to summarize, we demonstrated key tensor manipulations that are essential for deep learning workflows:

- **Loading and converting** the dataset into a tensor format.
- **Reshaping** tensors for specific batch sizes.
- **Slicing** tensors to select specific data portions.
- Performing **aggregation operations** like mean and sum.

- Using **broadcasting** to apply operations across the entire tensor efficiently.
- **Normalizing** the dataset to prepare it for training.

These tensor operations are fundamental building blocks in PyTorch and are vital for working with real-world data in deep learning applications.

Optimizing Tensor Computations on CUDA 12

When working with large datasets or complex deep learning models, the performance of tensor operations can become a bottleneck, particularly when using CPUs for processing. The leverage of **`CUDA 12`** to perform computations on a **`GPU`** can significantly speed up tensor manipulations to train models faster and handle larger amounts of data.

We now try to accelerate tensor computations on our previous sample program using **`CUDA 12`** by moving tensors to the GPU and performing various operations.

Moving Tensors to GPU

By default, tensors in PyTorch are created and processed on the CPU. However, to perform operations on a GPU, we need to explicitly move the tensors to the GPU using the **`.cuda()`** method.

We will start by moving the dataset to the GPU.

```
# Move the tensor to the GPU using CUDA

fish_tensor_gpu = fish_tensor.cuda()


print(f"Is the tensor on GPU? {fish_tensor_gpu.is_cuda}")
```

In the above, we use the **`.cuda()`** method to transfer the **`fish_tensor`** from the CPU to the **`GPU`**. The **`is_cuda`** attribute confirms that the tensor is now on the GPU.

Performing Tensor Operations on GPU

Once the tensor is on the GPU, we can perform the same operations as before, but with the significant performance benefit of using GPU acceleration.

Reshaping Tensor on GPU

Reshaping tensors is a common operation, especially when preparing batches of data for training. We have learned to do this in the previous topics.

```
# Reshape the tensor while it's on the GPU

reshaped_tensor_gpu = fish_tensor_gpu.view(-1, 2)

print(f"Reshaped Tensor (GPU) Shape:
{reshaped_tensor_gpu.shape}")
```

Slicing Tensor on the GPU

Slicing operations are frequently used to select specific portions of the data, and moving these computations to the GPU can improve performance when dealing with larger datasets.

```
# Slice the tensor while it's on the GPU

sliced_tensor_gpu = fish_tensor_gpu[:5, :3]

print(f"Sliced Tensor (GPU):\n{sliced_tensor_gpu}")
```

Since the slicing operation is now done on the GPU, it can be processed in parallel, enhancing performance compared to the CPU.

Aggregation on the GPU

Aggregation operations, such as calculating the mean and sum, benefit significantly from the GPU's parallelism. We will perform these operations on the GPU.

```
# Aggregation operations on the GPU (mean and sum)

mean_tensor_gpu = torch.mean(fish_tensor_gpu, dim=0)  #
Mean across each column

sum_tensor_gpu = torch.sum(fish_tensor_gpu, dim=1)    #
Sum across each row


print(f"Mean Tensor (GPU): {mean_tensor_gpu}")

print(f"Sum Tensor (GPU): {sum_tensor_gpu}")
```

Performing these operations on a GPU, especially for larger datasets, can lead to substantial speed improvements over CPU-based operations. The GPU's parallel architecture allows it to handle aggregation across large dimensions efficiently.

Broadcasting on GPU

Broadcasting, which involves applying operations to tensors of different shapes, can be accelerated by running on the GPU. We will add a scalar value to all elements of the tensor while it's on the GPU.

```
# Perform broadcasting on the GPU

scalar_gpu = torch.tensor(10.0).cuda()

broadcasted_tensor_gpu = fish_tensor_gpu + scalar_gpu

print(f"Broadcasted Tensor
(GPU):\n{broadcasted_tensor_gpu}")
```

With CUDA, broadcasting operations can be parallelized across thousands of GPU cores, making this operation significantly faster than on a CPU.

Normalizing Data on GPU

Normalization, which is commonly performed as a preprocessing step before feeding data into a neural network, can also benefit from GPU acceleration.

```
# Normalize the tensor on the GPU (mean = 0, std = 1)

mean_gpu = fish_tensor_gpu.mean(dim=0, keepdim=True)

std_gpu = fish_tensor_gpu.std(dim=0, keepdim=True)

normalized_tensor_gpu = (fish_tensor_gpu - mean_gpu) /
std_gpu


print(f"Normalized Tensor
(GPU):\n{normalized_tensor_gpu}")
```

By performing normalization directly on the GPU, you can significantly reduce the preprocessing time, especially for large datasets.

Measuring Performance Speedup on GPU

Here, we can measure the time taken to perform operations on the CPU versus the GPU. PyTorch provides a utility to measure the time spent on operations, which helps to highlight the speedup gained by using a GPU.

```
import time


# Timing tensor operations on CPU

start_cpu = time.time()

mean_tensor_cpu = torch.mean(fish_tensor, dim=0)  # Mean
on CPU

end_cpu = time.time()


cpu_time = end_cpu - start_cpu

print(f"Time taken for mean on CPU: {cpu_time:.6f}
seconds")


# Timing tensor operations on GPU

start_gpu = time.time()

mean_tensor_gpu = torch.mean(fish_tensor_gpu, dim=0)  #
Mean on GPU

end_gpu = time.time()
```

```
gpu_time = end_gpu - start_gpu

print(f"Time taken for mean on GPU: {gpu_time:.6f}
seconds")


speedup = cpu_time / gpu_time

print(f"Speedup by using GPU: {speedup:.2f}x")
```

This code compares the time taken to compute the mean of the Fish Dataset on both the CPU and GPU. You can expect the GPU to be much faster, especially for large datasets, showcasing the power of CUDA 12 in accelerating tensor operations.

Advanced Tensor Operations

Advanced tensor manipulations such as **stacking**, **squeezing/unsqueezing**, and **permuting** tensors are of much help while working with complex models, as most of these operations provide flexibility in preparing and transforming data to fit the requirements of various neural network architectures.

Stacking Tensors

Stacking allows multiple tensors to be combined along a new dimension, which is useful when batching data or combining outputs from different sources. It differs from concatenation, where tensors are joined along an existing dimension.

Here, we assume to have multiple slices of the dataset representing different batches. We can stack these slices along a new dimension to create a multi-dimensional tensor.

```
# Assume we have three tensor slices representing batches

batch1 = fish_tensor[:5]  # First 5 rows

batch2 = fish_tensor[5:10]  # Next 5 rows

batch3 = fish_tensor[10:15]  # Next 5 rows
```

```
# Stack the batches along a new dimension (axis 0)

stacked_tensor = torch.stack([batch1, batch2, batch3],
dim=0)

print(f"Shape of stacked tensor: {stacked_tensor.shape}")
```

In the above script:

- Each batch has a shape of **(5, 6)** (assuming 6 features per row).
- After stacking, the tensor gains a new dimension at the start, with a final shape of **(3, 5, 6)**, where **3** represents the number of batches.

This operation is particularly helpful when you need to combine multiple datasets or results from different sources while maintaining the separation between them.

Squeezing and Unsqueezing Tensors

In some situations, tensors may have extra dimensions of size 1 that are not required for computations. This is where **squeezing** and **unsqueezing** come in. Squeezing removes unnecessary dimensions, while unsqueezing adds new ones to fit specific layers or models.

Squeezing Tensors

Squeezing removes dimensions of size 1, simplifying the structure of the tensor.

```
# Create a tensor with an extra dimension

tensor_with_extra_dim = fish_tensor.unsqueeze(0)  #
Adding a dimension at axis 0

print(f"Original Shape (With Extra Dimension):
{tensor_with_extra_dim.shape}")


# Squeeze the tensor to remove the extra dimension

squeezed_tensor = torch.squeeze(tensor_with_extra_dim)

print(f"Squeezed Tensor Shape: {squeezed_tensor.shape}")
```

In the above, a new dimension is added to the start of the tensor, changing its shape from **(150, 6)** to **(1, 150, 6)**. By squeezing, we remove this unnecessary dimension and return the tensor to its original shape.

Unsqueezing Tensors

In some cases, layers in a neural network may require additional dimensions, such as a batch size or channel dimension. In these cases, unsqueezing adds the necessary dimension.

```
# Unsqueeze to add a new dimension at axis 1

unsqueezed_tensor = fish_tensor.unsqueeze(1)

print(f"Unsqueezed Tensor Shape:
{unsqueezed_tensor.shape}")
```

This operation transforms the shape of the tensor from **(150, 6)** to **(150, 1, 6)**, which can be useful when preparing tensors for layers like batch normalization or fully connected layers.

Permuting Tensors

Permuting is another powerful operation that allows you to rearrange the dimensions of a tensor. This is particularly useful when working with multidimensional data like images, where you may need to change the order of dimensions to match the expected input of a model.

Permuting Dimensions

For instance, if we need to change the order of dimensions to match the input format for a CNN, we can use the **permute()** function.

```
# Permute the dimensions of the fish tensor

permuted_tensor = fish_tensor.permute(1, 0)  # Swap axis
0 and 1

print(f"Permuted Tensor Shape: {permuted_tensor.shape}")
```

In this example, the original shape is **(150, 6)**. By permuting, we swap the first and second dimensions, resulting in a new shape of **(6, 150)**.

Using Permute with Multidimensional Data

Permuting is commonly used with higher-dimensional data, such as images with batch and channel dimensions. We will assume our tensor represents image-like data, and we need to prepare it for a convolutional layer.

```
# Unsqueeze the tensor to add a channel dimension

fish_tensor_channels = fish_tensor.unsqueeze(1)  # Shape: (150, 1, 6)


# Permute the tensor to place the channel last (if required)

permuted_tensor_channels = fish_tensor_channels.permute(0, 2, 1)

print(f"Permuted Tensor Shape (Channels Last): {permuted_tensor_channels.shape}")
```

This transforms the tensor from **`(150, 1, 6)`** to **`(150, 6, 1)`**, which could be required when working with models expecting the channel as the last dimension rather than the first.

Combining Advanced Operations

In practice, these tensor operations are often combined to prepare data for complex deep learning models. For example, when working with CNNs or RNNs, you might need to stack tensors, squeeze or unsqueeze dimensions, and permute axes to get the data in the right shape for training.

```
# Example: Combining stacking, unsqueezing, and permuting

stacked_batches = torch.stack([fish_tensor[:10], fish_tensor[10:20], fish_tensor[20:30]], dim=0)  # Shape (3, 10, 6)

stacked_batches_unsqueezed = stacked_batches.unsqueeze(1)  # Add a channel dimension (Shape: 3, 1, 10, 6)
```

```
final_tensor = stacked_batches_unsqueezed.permute(0, 2,
3, 1)  # Change the order of dimensions (Shape: 3, 10, 6,
1)


print(f"Final Tensor Shape: {final_tensor.shape}")
```

This example demonstrates how we can stack slices of the dataset, add a new dimension to represent channels, and permute the dimensions to match the input format required by specific models. These advanced tensor operations allow you to manipulate data flexibly, ensuring that it fits the requirements of different neural network architectures.

Summary

By the end of this chapter, you gained a comprehensive understanding of tensors, a critical data structure in PyTorch. You explored the dimensionality of tensors and learned how to work with different types, such as scalars, vectors, and matrices. Practical examples helped you understand how to create and manipulate tensors through various operations, including arithmetic calculations, reshaping, slicing, and joining tensors.

Additionally, you learned about the significance of broadcasting and aggregation operations, which are crucial for efficiently performing calculations on tensors. You applied these operations to real-world data, which reinforced the importance of tensors in deep learning workflows. Advanced concepts like stacking, squeezing, and permuting tensors were introduced, allowing you to manipulate data to meet the specific requirements of deep learning models.

Finally, you explored how CUDA 12 can be leveraged to accelerate tensor operations, significantly improving computational efficiency. These skills are essential as you continue your journey in deep learning, building and training neural networks using PyTorch.

Chapter 3: Building Neural Networks with PyTorch

Overview

In this chapter, we will explore how to build neural networks using **`PyTorch`**, one of the most widely used deep learning frameworks. The chapter begins with an introduction to PyTorch's **`nn module`**, which provides the essential building blocks for constructing neural networks. This module allows you to define layers, loss functions, and optimization strategies, making it an integral part of model creation in PyTorch. By the end of this section, you will have a clear understanding of how PyTorch simplifies the process of building neural networks.

Following that, we will focus on constructing **`feedforward neural networks`**. These are some of the simplest types of networks, consisting of layers where information moves in one direction—from input to output. We will cover how to implement **`multi-layer perceptrons (MLPs)`**, which are the backbone of many predictive models. This foundational knowledge will set the stage for building more complex networks in subsequent sections. The chapter then moves on to more advanced architectures, starting with **`CNNs`**, which are particularly effective for image recognition tasks. You will learn how CNNs process spatial data, extracting important features from images using convolutional layers. Next, we will dive into **`RNNs`**, designed for handling sequential data such as time series or text, where information needs to be retained across inputs.

Finally, we introduce the concept of **`transformer models and attention mechanisms`**, which have become pivotal in modern **`NLP`** tasks. You will explore how attention mechanisms enable models to focus on relevant parts of input data, improving performance in tasks like machine translation and text summarization. By the end of this chapter, you will be equipped with the knowledge to implement and experiment with a variety of neural network architectures using PyTorch.

Introduction to PyTorch's nn Module

The **`nn module`** in PyTorch is the core building block for constructing neural networks. It provides a high-level interface that abstracts much of the complexity involved in building and training models. At its heart, the **`nn`** module allows you to define layers of a neural network, manage forward and backward propagation, and apply various transformations to your data. This simplifies the process of implementing neural networks, making it easier to focus on the model's architecture rather than the underlying mechanics.

nn.Module Class

One of the key components in the **`nn module`** is the **`nn.Module`** class, from which all neural network layers inherit. This class serves as a base for creating your own layers or using predefined ones. It provides mechanisms for registering layers, keeping track of parameters, and defining the

forward pass, where the input is transformed through the network. For example, layers like **fully connected layers (nn.Linear)**, **convolutional layers (nn.Conv2d)**, and **recurrent layers (nn.RNN)** are all built using this fundamental module. When constructing a network, you subclass **nn.Module** and implement the forward method to define how data passes through your custom network.

Predefined Layers

Another essential part of the **nn** module is its suite of **predefined layers**, which serve as the building blocks of any neural network architecture. These include:

- **nn.Linear** for fully connected layers, where every input node is connected to every output node.
- **nn.Conv2d** for convolutional layers, which are commonly used in image processing tasks to capture spatial hierarchies by applying convolution filters.
- **nn.RNN**, **nn.LSTM**, and **nn.GRU** for recurrent layers, useful in processing sequential data like time series or text.
- **nn.BatchNorm** for batch normalization, which normalizes the output of a previous activation layer by scaling and shifting the data.

Activation Functions

Each of these layers provides flexibility in designing your neural network, and you can easily customize how data flows through the model by chaining these layers together. The **nn** module not only helps define the structure of the network but also offers a vast array of **activation functions** that introduce non-linearity into the network, which is crucial for enabling the network to learn complex patterns in the data. These include:

- **nn.ReLU** (Rectified Linear Unit), the most common activation function in deep learning, which introduces non-linearity by converting negative values to zero while leaving positive values unchanged.
- **nn.Sigmoid**, which squashes the input into a range between 0 and 1, often used in binary classification tasks.
- **nn.Tanh**, which scales inputs between -1 and 1, and is often used in networks where the output needs to vary across a broader range.

Loss Functions

In addition to layers and activations, the **nn** module simplifies the management of **loss functions**. PyTorch's **nn** module provides various loss functions that are essential in training neural networks, as they measure how far off the network's predictions are from the actual values. The module includes:

- **nn.CrossEntropyLoss**, typically used for classification tasks where the output represents probabilities over multiple classes.
- **nn.MSELoss** (Mean Squared Error Loss), often used for regression tasks where the output is continuous.
- **nn.NLLLoss** (Negative Log-Likelihood Loss), commonly paired with the softmax function for multi-class classification tasks.

Once the network structure and loss function are defined, PyTorch's **nn** module works seamlessly with the **torch.optim** module for **optimizers**, which adjust the network's weights during training to minimize the loss. Common optimizers like **SGD** (Stochastic Gradient Descent) and **Adam** are easily integrated into the training loop, allowing for flexible updates of the network's parameters.

Beyond these foundational components, the **nn** module is highly flexible and modular, enabling the construction of a wide range of neural networks, from simple to highly complex architectures. Current trends in neural network design demonstrate the versatility of the **nn** module across different types of models.

One widely used architecture is the **feedforward neural network (FNN)**, which consists of multiple layers where data flows in a single direction, from input to output. FNNs are often implemented for basic classification and regression tasks, where data is processed through several fully connected layers. These types of networks can be built using simple components like **nn.Linear** and **nn.ReLU**, and are foundational in many introductory deep learning tasks.

In more complex domains like **image recognition**, **CNNs** are commonly constructed using the **nn.Conv2d** layer. CNNs are designed to automatically and adaptively learn spatial hierarchies in images, making them highly effective for tasks like object detection, segmentation, and image classification. CNNs use convolutional layers to detect local features like edges and textures, pooling layers to reduce the dimensionality, and fully connected layers to classify the extracted features. These networks are not only powerful but also computationally efficient, making them suitable for real-time applications like autonomous driving and medical image analysis.

Another trend is the rise of **RNNs**, which are especially useful for handling sequential data such as time series, speech, or text. RNNs, along with their advanced variants like **LSTMs** and **GRUs**, can be easily built using **nn.RNN**, **nn.LSTM**, and **nn.GRU**. These architectures allow information to persist across time steps, capturing dependencies in sequential data. For example, RNNs and LSTMs are widely used in NLP for tasks like language translation, text generation, and sentiment analysis. In recent years, researchers have begun combining CNNs and RNNs to handle tasks that involve both spatial and temporal data, such as video processing.

One of the most significant trends in modern neural network design is the use of **transformer models**, which have revolutionized natural language processing and other fields. Transformers rely heavily on **attention mechanisms**, which allow the model to focus on relevant parts of the input data while processing it. This is particularly useful in tasks like machine translation, where each word in a sentence depends on the context of the entire sentence. PyTorch's **nn** module provides tools for implementing transformer models through layers like **nn.Transformer** and **nn.MultiheadAttention**. These layers form the basis of highly successful models like **BERT (Bidirectional Encoder Representations from Transformers)** and **GPT (Generative Pretrained Transformers)**, which have set new benchmarks in NLP tasks.

The flexibility of the **nn** module extends beyond these popular architectures. It also supports custom layers and architectures, allowing researchers to experiment with new ideas and prototype novel neural networks. By subclassing **nn.Module**, you can implement any layer or operation that may not be readily available in PyTorch's standard library. This flexibility has contributed to PyTorch's rapid adoption in both academia and industry, where innovation often demands highly customizable neural networks.

The **nn** module's integration with the broader PyTorch ecosystem—such as **automatic differentiation** with **torch.autograd**, **GPU acceleration** with CUDA, and the **DataLoader** for efficient data handling—makes it a complete framework for neural network construction. Whether you are building a simple feedforward network or a state-of-the-art transformer model, the PyTorch **nn** module provides the necessary tools to build, train, and deploy your models efficiently.

Feedforward Neural Networks

Feedforward Neural Networks (FNNs) are among the simplest types of neural networks, yet they are the foundation for many advanced architectures. In these networks, information flows in one direction—from the input layer through the hidden layers to the output layer—without looping back. Each layer in a feedforward network is fully connected to the next, meaning every neuron in one layer is connected to every neuron in the subsequent layer. FNNs have been widely used in various real-world applications, particularly in tasks like **classification** and **regression**. Their simple yet powerful structure makes them effective for problems where the relationship between the input and output is direct.

Feedforward Neural Networks in Real-World Applications

Feedforward neural networks are applied in numerous domains. One popular application is in **image classification**, where an FNN is trained to recognize different objects in an image. Though more advanced architectures like CNNs (Convolutional Neural Networks) are usually employed for complex image tasks, FNNs are still effective for smaller, less complex datasets. Another common use of FNNs is in **regression tasks**, where the network predicts a continuous output based on input data. Examples of regression tasks include predicting housing prices based on features like size, location, and number of bedrooms or predicting stock prices using historical financial data.

In fields like **medical diagnosis**, feedforward networks are used to classify diseases based on patient data, such as symptoms, medical history, and test results. The network is trained on a labeled dataset where the input features are patient records, and the output is the diagnosis. FNNs are also utilized in **fraud detection**, where the network is trained to classify transactions as fraudulent or legitimate based on historical transaction data.

In general, FNNs excel at problems where the input-output mapping is relatively simple and does not require the model to retain past information (as is the case in sequential models like RNNs). This makes FNNs suitable for static, non-sequential data.

Designing a Simple Feedforward Neural Network

To better understand how a feedforward neural network operates, we will demonstrate how to design and train a simple FNN using the **Fish Dataset** we have been working with. Our goal will be to predict a target variable based on the features in the dataset. In this demonstration, we will assume the target is a regression task, such as predicting the weight of the fish based on other features like length, height, and species.

Defining Feedforward Neural Network

To design the network, we will define a class that extends **nn.Module**, which is the base class for all neural networks in PyTorch. In this simple feedforward neural network, we will use a few fully connected (linear) layers, followed by activation functions.

```
import torch.nn as nn


# Define the Feedforward Neural Network

class FishNet(nn.Module):

   def __init__(self, input_size, hidden_size,
output_size):

       super(FishNet, self).__init__()

       # First hidden layer

       self.fc1 = nn.Linear(input_size, hidden_size)
```

```
        # Second hidden layer
        self.fc2 = nn.Linear(hidden_size, hidden_size)
        # Output layer
        self.output = nn.Linear(hidden_size, output_size)
        # Activation function
        self.relu = nn.ReLU()

    def forward(self, x):
        # First hidden layer with activation
        x = self.relu(self.fc1(x))
        # Second hidden layer with activation
        x = self.relu(self.fc2(x))
        # Output layer (no activation here since it's a
regression task)
        x = self.output(x)
        return x

# Set input, hidden, and output sizes
input_size = X_train_tensor.shape[1]  # Number of
features
hidden_size = 64  # Can be adjusted
output_size = 1  # Regression task (predicting one value)
```

In this above architecture:

- **`fc1`**: The first fully connected layer takes the input features and outputs to the hidden layer.
- **`fc2`**: The second hidden layer processes the output of the first layer.
- **`output`**: The final output layer predicts the target variable.
- **Activation function (`ReLU`)**: A rectified linear unit is applied after each hidden layer to introduce non-linearity.

This whole structure forms a simple multi-layer perceptron (MLP), which can effectively learn patterns in the data for regression tasks.

Training the Neural Network

Now that the network is defined, we can train it using the training data. We will define a loss function (mean squared error for regression) and an optimizer (Adam, for efficient weight updates). Then, we will implement the training loop.

```
# Initialize the model, loss function, and optimizer

model = FishNet(input_size, hidden_size, output_size)

criterion = nn.MSELoss()  # Mean Squared Error Loss for
regression

optimizer = torch.optim.Adam(model.parameters(),
lr=0.001)


# Training loop

num_epochs = 100

for epoch in range(num_epochs):

   model.train()  # Set the model to training mode

   optimizer.zero_grad()  # Zero the gradients


   # Forward pass
```

```
    outputs = model(X_train_tensor)

    loss = criterion(outputs, y_train_tensor.unsqueeze(1))
# Reshape y to match output size


    # Backward pass and optimization

    loss.backward()

    optimizer.step()


    # Print the loss at certain intervals

    if (epoch+1) % 10 == 0:

        print(f'Epoch [{epoch+1}/{num_epochs}], Loss:
{loss.item():.4f}')
```

Key points to remember in the training loop:

- **`model.train()`**: Puts the model in training mode, allowing for backpropagation.
- **Forward pass**: The input data is passed through the network, and predictions are made.
- **Loss function**: The error between the predictions and actual target values is calculated using mean squared error (MSE).
- **Backward pass**: The gradients of the loss function with respect to the network's parameters are computed.
- **Optimizer step**: The optimizer updates the network weights to minimize the loss.

Evaluating the Model

After training, we can evaluate the model on the test set to see how well it generalizes to unseen data. For this, we will calculate the predictions on the test data and compute the loss using the same criterion.

```
model.eval()  # Set the model to evaluation mode
```

```
with torch.no_grad():  # No need to compute gradients
during evaluation

   test_outputs = model(X_test_tensor)

   test_loss = criterion(test_outputs,
y_test_tensor.unsqueeze(1))

   print(f'Test Loss: {test_loss.item():.4f}')
```

In evaluation mode, the network parameters remain fixed, and no backpropagation or weight updates occur. The performance on the test data gives us an indication of how well the model has learned from the training data.

Predicting New Data

Once the network is trained, you can use it to make predictions on new, unseen data. Suppose we have a new set of fish measurements and want to predict the target variable.

```
new_data = torch.tensor([[23.5, 10.2, 3.5, 1.2, 5.0,
2.3]], dtype=torch.float32)  # Example data

new_data_normalized =
torch.tensor(scaler.transform(new_data))  # Apply the
same scaling used during training


# Predict the output using the trained model

model.eval()

with torch.no_grad():

   prediction = model(new_data_normalized)

   print(f'Predicted Target: {prediction.item():.4f}')
```

This simple feedforward network can now be used to make predictions on any new data. The model takes in features, processes them through its layers, and outputs a prediction based on the learned patterns from the training data.

Building CNNs

CNNs have become a staple in modern deep learning, particularly for tasks involving image recognition, object detection, and other tasks requiring spatial understanding of data. CNNs are designed to automatically and adaptively learn spatial hierarchies by applying filters (convolutions) that capture low-level features like edges and gradients, and progressively learn more complex patterns such as textures, shapes, and even whole objects. This makes CNNs highly effective for image processing tasks, though they are also being adapted for time series and other structured data in certain cases.

Unlike feedforward neural networks, which connect every neuron in one layer to every neuron in the next, CNNs employ a **convolutional operation** that focuses on smaller regions of input data, reducing the computational burden and allowing the network to capture local patterns in the data. This design also allows CNNs to maintain translation invariance, meaning they can recognize features in different parts of an image or dataset regardless of their location.

Structure of Convolutional Neural Networks

CNNs are composed of several layers, each designed to perform specific functions. Below are some common layers you will encounter when building CNNs:

- **Convolutional Layers**: These layers apply convolution operations using filters (also called kernels) that slide over the input data and perform element-wise multiplications. The result of these multiplications is summed up to form a feature map, which helps the network detect local patterns in the data.
- **Activation Function (ReLU)**: After the convolutional layer, a non-linear activation function like ReLU (Rectified Linear Unit) is applied to introduce non-linearity, which helps the network capture complex patterns.
- **Pooling Layers**: Pooling layers reduce the spatial dimensions of the data by taking the maximum (max pooling) or average (average pooling) of a subset of the data. This reduces the computational complexity and helps the network focus on the most important features.
- **Fully Connected Layers**: After the data passes through the convolutional and pooling layers, it is flattened into a vector and fed into fully connected layers, similar to feedforward neural networks. These layers combine the learned features to make predictions or classifications.

CNNs in Today's Use

CNNs are widely used in computer vision tasks. In **image classification**, CNNs can identify objects in images by learning different features at different layers, from edges in the first layers to complete objects in the deeper layers. In **object detection**, CNNs can not only classify objects but also locate them in an image by drawing bounding boxes around the objects. In healthcare, CNNs are used for **medical imaging**, such as detecting anomalies in X-rays, CT scans, or MRIs. CNNs are also used in **self-driving cars** to detect road signs, pedestrians, and other vehicles.

While CNNs are predominantly applied in image processing, they are also used in other fields, such as speech recognition and time-series analysis, where the data exhibits some form of spatial or temporal structure.

Designing CNN

Now, we will build a simple CNN. Since our dataset is not image-based, we will treat it as a structured dataset with multiple features. Although CNNs are typically designed for image data, we can still create a CNN-like structure to process the tabular data, using 1D convolutions to capture patterns across features. The goal here is to demonstrate the flexibility of CNNs, even when the data is not image-based.

Since the focus is on building a CNN, we will assume the data has already been preprocessed and is ready for use in tensor format (as likely done in the previous section).

Defining the Convolutional Neural Network

The CNN for this task will consist of 1D convolutional layers, followed by pooling layers, and will eventually flatten the features before passing them through fully connected layers.

Below is a simple CNN architecture for the same Fish Dataset.

```
import torch.nn as nn


# Define the CNN

class FishCNN(nn.Module):

    def __init__(self, input_channels, output_size):

        super(FishCNN, self).__init__()

        # 1D Convolutional layer (input channels, output
channels, kernel size)
```

```
        self.conv1 = nn.Conv1d(in_channels=input_channels,
out_channels=32, kernel_size=3)

        self.conv2 = nn.Conv1d(in_channels=32,
out_channels=64, kernel_size=3)

        self.pool = nn.MaxPool1d(kernel_size=2)  # Pooling
layer

        self.fc1 = nn.Linear(64 * 2, 128)  # Fully
connected layer (adjust input size)

        self.fc2 = nn.Linear(128, output_size)  # Output
layer


        self.relu = nn.ReLU()  # Activation function


    def forward(self, x):

        # Convolutional layers with activation and pooling

        x = self.pool(self.relu(self.conv1(x)))

        x = self.pool(self.relu(self.conv2(x)))


        # Flatten the output from the convolutional layers

        x = x.view(-1, 64 * 2)  # Adjust the size based on
the input

        # Fully connected layers

        x = self.relu(self.fc1(x))
```

```
        x = self.fc2(x)  # No activation here, regression
task

        return x


# Set the input size and output size

input_channels = 1  # We will treat each row of the
dataset as a 1D input

output_size = 1  # Regression task (predicting one value)
```

In the above CNN architecture,

- **`conv1` and `conv2`**: These are the 1D convolutional layers that apply filters over the input data. The kernel size defines the size of the filter, which slides over the data, detecting local patterns. In this case, we use two convolutional layers, with the first layer extracting 32 feature maps and the second extracting 64 feature maps.
- **Max Pooling (`pool`)**: After each convolutional layer, we apply max pooling to reduce the dimensionality and focus on the most important features. Max pooling reduces the input size by half, which makes the model more computationally efficient.
- **Fully Connected Layers**: After the data has passed through the convolutional and pooling layers, it is flattened into a 1D vector and fed into fully connected layers, just like in a feedforward network. These layers combine the learned features and produce the final output.
- **Activation Function (ReLU)**: We use the ReLU activation function after each convolutional and fully connected layer, introducing non-linearity to the model.

This CNN processes the input data through the convolutional layers and reduces the dimensionality via pooling before making predictions through fully connected layers. In this case, the predictions could be for a regression task, where we predict a continuous value based on the input features.

Evaluating CNN on Structured Data

Even though CNNs are primarily used for image or grid-like data, 1D convolutional layers allow us to apply CNNs to structured datasets. The network learns to capture local patterns in the feature set, which could represent relationships between the features of different fish in the dataset.

Given below is how you would run the forward pass of the network.

```
# Assuming X_train_tensor is the input tensor for
training data

model = FishCNN(input_channels=1, output_size=1)


# Reshape input tensor to match CNN input requirements
(batch_size, input_channels, input_length)

X_train_cnn = X_train_tensor.unsqueeze(1)  # Adding a
channel dimension

output = model(X_train_cnn)

print(output.shape)
```

The input data is reshaped to have an extra channel dimension because CNNs expect the input to have a batch size, number of channels, and input length. By applying 1D convolutions, the CNN extracts patterns along the feature axis of the dataset.

Recurrent Neural Networks (RNNs)

RNNs are a class of neural networks designed specifically for sequential data, where the order of data points plays a crucial role. Unlike feedforward networks, which assume independence between inputs, RNNs are built to recognize and retain patterns across sequences. They introduce the concept of loops, allowing information to persist through time steps by passing the hidden state from one time step to the next. This enables the network to capture dependencies across the sequence, making it ideal for tasks like time-series prediction, NLP, and other sequence-based data.

The core idea behind RNNs is their ability to maintain a hidden state that remembers information from previous inputs. In a traditional feedforward network, the output depends solely on the current input. However, in an RNN, the output depends not only on the current input but also on the hidden state that contains information from previous inputs. This structure allows RNNs to learn from temporal patterns, making them incredibly powerful for sequential data tasks.

Role of RNNs in Today's AI Development

In modern AI development, RNNs have been pivotal in areas such as **language modeling**,

speech recognition, **time-series analysis**, and **music generation**. For example, in **NLP**, RNNs are used to generate text, translate languages, and recognize speech, where understanding the sequence of words is critical. In **time-series forecasting**, RNNs have proven effective in predicting future values based on historical data, which is common in stock market prediction, weather forecasting, and other financial applications.

While RNNs have been extremely successful in sequential data modeling, they also suffer from limitations such as **vanishing gradients**, which makes it difficult to learn long-term dependencies in very long sequences. To address this, advanced variants like **LSTM** networks and **GRU** have been developed. These architectures introduce mechanisms like gates to control the flow of information, allowing the network to retain or forget information as needed over long sequences.

Despite their limitations, RNNs continue to play a crucial role in many AI systems, especially when combined with other architectures like **CNNs** and **Transformer models** for hybrid solutions. In recent years, **attention mechanisms** and **transformers** have become more prominent in tasks like NLP, but RNNs remain foundational in understanding sequential data.

Implementing RNNs

While RNNs are typically used for tasks where the order of data matters, such as text or time series, we can still demonstrate their functionality using our **Fish Dataset** by treating it as a sequence of features over time. This demonstration will help illustrate how RNNs can capture patterns across the data. In our case, each row can be treated as a sequence, and we will predict a target value based on that sequence.

Defining the Recurrent Neural Network

To implement an RNN, we will use the **nn.RNN** class from PyTorch. This class represents the core of the RNN architecture, allowing us to process sequential data one time step at a time. Given below is how we define a basic RNN:

```
import torch.nn as nn



# Define the RNN

class FishRNN(nn.Module):

    def __init__(self, input_size, hidden_size,
output_size, num_layers=1):
```

```
        super(FishRNN, self).__init__()
        self.hidden_size = hidden_size
        self.num_layers = num_layers

        # Define the RNN layer
        self.rnn = nn.RNN(input_size, hidden_size,
num_layers, batch_first=True)
        # Fully connected layer to output
        self.fc = nn.Linear(hidden_size, output_size)

    def forward(self, x):
        # Initialize hidden state with zeros (for the
first time step)
        h0 = torch.zeros(self.num_layers, x.size(0),
self.hidden_size).to(x.device)

        # Forward propagate the RNN
        out, _ = self.rnn(x, h0)  # Output from RNN and
the hidden state

        # Take the output from the last time step
        out = out[:, -1, :]  # We are only interested in
the final output
```

```
        # Pass through fully connected layer to predict
the target

        out = self.fc(out)

        return out


# Set input, hidden, and output sizes

input_size = X_train_tensor.shape[2]  # Number of
features (each "time step" will be a feature)

hidden_size = 64  # Number of units in the hidden layer

output_size = 1  # Regression task (predicting one value)
```

In the above RNN Architecture,

- **RNN Layer (`self.rnn`)**: The **`nn.RNN`** layer is where the recurrent operations happen. We define the input size (number of features), hidden size (number of units in the hidden layer), and the number of layers (how deep the RNN is). By setting **`batch_first=True`**, we indicate that the batch size is the first dimension in our input tensor.
- **Hidden State Initialization (`h0`)**: At each forward pass, the hidden state is initialized to zeros, and the RNN processes the input sequence step by step.
- **Fully Connected Layer (`self.fc`)**: After processing the sequence, we use the final hidden state (output of the last time step) to make a prediction. The fully connected layer takes this final hidden state and produces the output.

Processing the Data for RNNs

RNNs expect the data to be formatted as sequences. In our case, each row in the Fish Dataset is treated as a "time step," and the features in each row are processed sequentially. Here, we will reshape the input data to fit this requirement.

```
# Reshape input tensor to match RNN input requirements
(batch_size, sequence_length, input_size)
```

```
X_train_rnn = X_train_tensor.unsqueeze(1)  # Adding a sequence dimension (treating each feature as a sequence)

output = model(X_train_rnn)

print(output.shape)
```

This ensures that the data is in the correct format for the RNN to process.

Forward Pass and Predictions

Once the data is reshaped, the RNN processes the input sequences and makes predictions based on the final hidden state. The forward pass of the network remains similar to what we've seen in feedforward and convolutional networks, but the internal structure allows the RNN to "remember" previous inputs as it moves through the sequence.

```
# Initialize the RNN model

model = FishRNN(input_size=input_size, hidden_size=hidden_size, output_size=output_size)


# Forward pass (assuming X_train_tensor is the input tensor)

output = model(X_train_rnn)

print(output)
```

In the above, the RNN processes each row of the Fish Dataset sequentially, using the hidden state to retain information across the sequence.

RNN Model Evaluation

Once the forward pass is complete, the model can be evaluated to see how well it captures patterns in the data. This is particularly useful for time-series forecasting, speech recognition, or any other task where understanding the sequence of inputs is critical. Although CNNs and feedforward networks process data independently, RNNs excel at capturing temporal dependencies and patterns across time steps.

Summary

In this chapter, the focus was on understanding the different types of neural networks and how they were built using PyTorch's powerful **nn** module. Starting with the exploration of feedforward neural networks, the chapter explained how information flows in one direction, making these networks suitable for simpler tasks such as classification and regression. The process of building a simple feedforward neural network on the Fish Dataset demonstrated how PyTorch's basic components help in structuring such models. Next, CNNs were introduced, emphasizing their ability to recognize spatial patterns through convolutional layers. The example of constructing a CNN showed how these networks could be adapted for non-image datasets, using 1D convolutions to process structured data.

RNNs were then explored, with particular attention given to their role in handling sequential data. Their capacity to retain information over time through hidden states was highlighted, and an example was provided to showcase how an RNN could be implemented to detect patterns across sequences. The chapter also touched on the real-world applications of these networks in tasks like time-series forecasting and natural language processing. By the end, a foundational understanding of how different neural network architectures, including feedforward, CNNs, and RNNs, are constructed using PyTorch had been established, allowing you to grasp your specific use cases and basic implementations.

CHAPTER 4: TRAINING NEURAL NETWORKS

CHAPTER 4: TRAINING NEURAL NETWORKS

Overview

In this chapter, the focus will be on how neural networks are trained effectively using PyTorch, moving beyond just model design. We will begin by understanding the **`PyTorch training workflow`**, which outlines the essential steps involved in setting up and training a model. This will provide a clear process for moving from defining a model to adjusting its parameters to minimize error. Through this, you will learn how training cycles are structured, and how models learn from the data.

Next, the chapter will explore **`optimizers and learning rate scheduling`**, which are critical components in training neural networks. We will learn how optimizers like Adam and SGD update model weights and how learning rate schedulers can adjust the learning pace during training to improve performance and stability. This is important for fine-tuning models to avoid common pitfalls like overfitting or underfitting. Further, we will cover **`gradient computations with CUDA 12`**, focusing on how PyTorch leverages GPU acceleration to handle large-scale models and datasets more efficiently. The role of CUDA in speeding up backpropagation through gradient calculations will be highlighted. Additionally, **`mixed precision training with AMP`** will be introduced, demonstrating how to combine float16 and float32 calculations to improve memory usage and accelerate training, particularly on GPUs.

Lastly, we will delve into **`using torch.profiler`** for training insights. This tool allows you to monitor and profile your training processes, offering detailed information on performance bottlenecks. By the end of the chapter, you will have a comprehensive understanding of how to train neural networks effectively, with the tools and techniques necessary to optimize the training process.

PyTorch Training Workflow

Training a neural network involves a structured workflow that revolves around three key operations: **`forward pass`**, **`backward pass`**, and **`weight updates`**. Understanding each of these steps is essential to effectively manage the entire training process. The process starts with feeding input data to the model, calculating predictions, and ends with updating the model's parameters based on the computed errors. Each component plays a specific role in enabling the model to learn from the data iteratively.

Forward Pass

The forward pass is the first step in training, where input data is passed through the model to generate predictions. During this phase, the data flows through the network's layers, starting from the input layer, moving through hidden layers, and finally arriving at the output layer. Each layer applies transformations, such as matrix multiplications and activation functions, on the input data to extract features and make predictions. The final output of the forward pass is typically compared to the ground truth labels to compute the **loss**, which quantifies how far off the model's predictions are from the actual values.

The forward pass primarily involves:

- Processing data through the model's layers.
- Using activation functions to introduce non-linearity.
- Producing the output, which can be used to calculate the loss.

Loss Function

The loss function plays a central role in training. It measures how far the predicted values are from the actual target values. The type of loss function depends on the task: for classification tasks, **cross-entropy loss** is typically used, whereas for regression tasks, **mean squared error (MSE)** is common. The output of the loss function directs how the model's parameters (weights) need to be adjusted. The smaller the loss, the better the model's predictions are. The loss function is also crucial for calculating the gradients during the backward pass.

Backward Pass (Backpropagation)

Once the forward pass has produced a loss, the next step is the backward pass, which uses a technique called **backpropagation**. Backpropagation involves calculating the gradients of the loss function with respect to the model's weights and biases. These gradients tell the optimizer how the weights need to change to reduce the error in subsequent iterations. In PyTorch, backpropagation is triggered by calling **loss.backward()**. PyTorch automatically computes these gradients using the **autograd** engine, which tracks the operations performed on the tensors.

Key steps in the backward pass:

- Calculating gradients for each weight and bias using the chain rule.
- Storing the gradients to be used during the weight update step.

The backward pass ensures that the network learns by adjusting the parameters in the direction that reduces the loss.

Updating Weights

Once the gradients are calculated, they are passed to the **optimizer**, which updates the weights and biases of the model based on the learning rate and the computed gradients. This is where the model's parameters are adjusted to minimize the loss. The learning rate controls how big or small the weight adjustments are in each iteration. If the learning rate is too large, the model may converge too quickly to a suboptimal solution. If it's too small, the training process can be excessively slow and may not converge at all.

In PyTorch, the most common optimizers are **`Stochastic Gradient Descent (SGD)`** and **`Adam`**, both of which update the weights iteratively using the gradients. After each update, the forward and backward passes are repeated with the updated weights until the model reaches an acceptable level of accuracy or until a predefined number of epochs is completed.

Key areas in the weight update process:

- Using optimizers like SGD or Adam to adjust model parameters.
- Applying the learning rate to control the step size of the updates.
- Iteratively refining the model to reduce the error over time.

Epochs and Batches

The process of forward pass, backward pass, and weight updates is repeated multiple times during training, each time with a new mini-batch of data. An **`epoch`** is defined as one complete pass through the entire training dataset. In most cases, the dataset is divided into **`mini-batches`** to make the training more efficient and to allow the gradients to be updated more frequently. Instead of calculating the loss and updating the weights for the entire dataset at once, mini-batch training divides the dataset into smaller chunks, speeding up the process and improving generalization.

- **Mini-batch size** determines how many samples are processed before updating the model's weights. A larger batch size gives a more accurate gradient estimate but requires more memory.
- The number of **epochs** defines how many times the training algorithm will work through the entire training dataset. More epochs allow the model to learn better but also increase the risk of overfitting.

Key Factors affecting Neural Network Training

During the training process, there are several factors that have a significant impact on the effectiveness and efficiency of the neural network learning process. These factors include:

Factor	Description
`Learning Rate`	Determines the size of the weight updates after each iteration. A high learning rate may cause the model to converge too quickly to a poor solution.
`Optimizer Choice`	Different optimizers (SGD, Adam) affect how the weights are updated and can impact both the speed and accuracy of learning.

Loss Function	The choice of loss function depends on the type of task (classification vs regression) and influences the direction of the updates.
Batch Size	Larger batches provide more accurate gradient estimates but require more memory and can slow down the training process.
Number of Epochs	The number of complete passes through the training dataset. Too few epochs may underfit, while too many can lead to overfitting.
Gradient Computation	Efficient backpropagation ensures faster training. When using a GPU (CUDA), gradient computations are accelerated, making the process faster.
Weight Initialization	Improper initialization can lead to vanishing or exploding gradients, causing the model to struggle with learning.
Regularization	Methods like dropout and weight decay help prevent overfitting by penalizing large weights and making the model more generalizable.

Each of these factors needs to be considered during training to ensure that the neural network learns effectively and generalizes well to unseen data. Additionally, **GPU acceleration with CUDA** can significantly speed up training by performing matrix operations and gradient calculations in parallel.

Sample Program: Training Neural Networks

Here now, we will demonstrate to train the neural network created in the previous chapter. The network structure has already been built, so we will focus on preparing the training loop, performing the forward pass, backpropagation, and updating weights to minimize the loss. We will leverage the key components of PyTorch for training, including the loss function, optimizer, and gradient updates.

Defining Training Components

Since the model and dataset have already been defined in the previous chapter, we will jump straight into defining the components needed for training. These include:

- **Loss function**: In this case, we will use **mean squared error (MSE)** since we are working on a regression task (predicting a continuous value).
- **Optimizer**: We will use **Adam**, a popular optimizer that adapts the learning rate during training to improve convergence.

```
# Initialize the model (assuming FishNet model from previous chapter)

model = FishNet(input_size, hidden_size, output_size)



# Define the loss function and optimizer

criterion = torch.nn.MSELoss()  # Mean Squared Error Loss for regression

optimizer = torch.optim.Adam(model.parameters(), lr=0.001)  # Adam optimizer with a learning rate of 0.001
```

In the above, we define the **`MSELoss`** function, which will compute the error between the predicted values and the actual target values. The **`Adam optimizer`** is responsible for updating the model's weights based on the computed gradients during training.

Defining Training Loop

The training loop is where the actual learning takes place. For each epoch, the loop performs the following steps:

- Perform a **forward pass** to generate predictions from the model.
- Compute the **loss** by comparing the predictions to the actual target values.
- Perform a **backward pass** to calculate the gradients.
- Update the model's weights using the optimizer.

```
# Set the number of epochs

num_epochs = 100



# Training loop
```

```
for epoch in range(num_epochs):
    model.train()  # Set the model to training mode

    optimizer.zero_grad()  # Clear the previous gradients

    # Forward pass: Generate predictions
    outputs = model(X_train_tensor)

    # Compute the loss
    loss = criterion(outputs, y_train_tensor.unsqueeze(1))
# Ensure the target has the correct shape

    # Backward pass: Compute gradients
    loss.backward()

    # Update weights
    optimizer.step()

    # Print loss every 10 epochs
    if (epoch + 1) % 10 == 0:
        print(f'Epoch [{epoch+1}/{num_epochs}], Loss:
{loss.item():.4f}')
```

Following are the key steps in Training Loop:

- **model.train()**: Sets the model in training mode, ensuring that all layers, especially those like batch normalization or dropout, behave accordingly.
- **Forward pass**: The model generates predictions (**outputs**) by passing the training data (**X_train_tensor**) through the neural network.
- **Loss computation**: The **MSELoss** function compares the model's predictions (**outputs**) with the actual target values (**y_train_tensor**), calculating how far the predictions are from the true values.
- **Backward pass**: Calling **loss.backward()** calculates the gradients of the loss with respect to the model's parameters (weights). These gradients tell the model in which direction (and by how much) to adjust the weights to reduce the loss.
- **Weight update**: The optimizer updates the model's parameters using the computed gradients and the learning rate, moving the weights in the direction that minimizes the loss.

The training loop iterates through the dataset multiple times (one pass through the entire dataset is called an **epoch**). As the loop progresses, the loss should gradually decrease, indicating that the model is learning.

Evaluating Model

After the model has been trained, it's important to evaluate its performance on unseen data. This helps in understanding how well the model generalizes to new data. During evaluation, we set the model to **evaluation mode**, which disables certain layers like dropout (if used), ensuring consistent behavior.

```
# Set the model to evaluation mode

model.eval()


# Disable gradient computation during evaluation

with torch.no_grad():

    # Forward pass on the test data

    test_outputs = model(X_test_tensor)
```

```
    # Compute the test loss

    test_loss = criterion(test_outputs,
y_test_tensor.unsqueeze(1))


    print(f'Test Loss: {test_loss.item():.4f}')
```

In the above script, **model.eval()** is used to switch the model to evaluation mode, ensuring that layers such as dropout behave differently compared to training mode. The **torch.no_grad()** context disables gradient calculation since we don't need it during inference or evaluation. The test loss gives an indication of how well the model performs on unseen data.

Saving Trained Model

Once training is complete, you may want to save the model for future use, especially if the model will be deployed or used for inference on new data. PyTorch allows you to save the model's state, which includes the learned weights.

```
# Save the model's state_dict (the model's learned
parameters)

torch.save(model.state_dict(), 'fish_model.pth')
```

This saves the trained model's parameters in a file called **fish_model.pth**. The **state_dict** contains all the learnable parameters (weights and biases) of the model.

Loading Saved Model

If you later need to load the saved model and perform inference on new data, you can reload the model and its parameters as follows:

```
# Initialize the model structure

model = FishNet(input_size, hidden_size, output_size)
```

```
# Load the model's parameters
model.load_state_dict(torch.load('fish_model.pth'))


# Set the model to evaluation mode
model.eval()
```

After loading the model's parameters, you can use the model to make predictions on new data or evaluate it further.

Making Predictions on New Data

Once the model is trained and evaluated, you can use it to make predictions on new, unseen data. Given below is how to pass a new example through the model to get predictions.

```
# Example of new fish data (normalized)
new_data = torch.tensor([[23.5, 10.2, 3.5, 1.2, 5.0, 2.3]], dtype=torch.float32)


# Pass through the trained model to get predictions
model.eval()
with torch.no_grad():
    prediction = model(new_data)
    print(f'Predicted value: {prediction.item():.4f}')
```

In this case, we've passed a single new sample of fish data through the trained model to predict a target value. Since the model is already trained, there's no need to calculate gradients, so we use **torch.no_grad()** to disable gradient computation during inference. This hands-on demonstration of training a neural network showcases the key steps involved in the process.

Optimizers and Learning Rate Scheduling

Optimizers control how the model's weights are adjusted during each iteration of the training loop. In essence, optimizers direct the process of minimizing the loss function by modifying the weights and biases of the neural network based on the gradients calculated during backpropagation. The choice of optimizer can significantly affect the convergence speed and performance of a model. Two of the most popular optimizers in PyTorch are **`Stochastic Gradient Descent (SGD)`** and **`Adam`**. These optimizers have their own strengths, and choosing between them often depends on the specific problem and dataset.

Stochastic Gradient Descent (SGD)

`Stochastic Gradient Descent (SGD)` is one of the simplest and most commonly used optimization algorithms. It updates the model's weights by calculating the gradient of the loss function with respect to the model's parameters and then moving the weights in the direction that reduces the loss. This movement is scaled by a factor called the **`learning rate`**, which controls the size of the step taken in the parameter space.

The general update rule for SGD is:

$$\theta = \theta - \eta \cdot \nabla J(\theta)$$

Where:

- θ represents the model's parameters (weights and biases).
- η is the learning rate.
- $\nabla J(\theta)$ is the gradient of the loss function with respect to the parameters.

In traditional gradient descent, the update is made using the entire dataset, which can be computationally expensive. **`Stochastic`** gradient descent, however, updates the weights based on a mini-batch of the data, making the training process faster. This stochastic nature introduces noise, which helps the model to avoid local minima, though it may also cause oscillations around the optimum.

Adaptive Moment Estimation (Adam)

`Adam` is a more sophisticated optimization algorithm that combines the benefits of **`AdaGrad`** and **`RMSProp`**. It adjusts the learning rate for each parameter individually by computing adaptive learning rates using estimates of both the first and second moments of the gradients. Adam calculates running averages of the gradients (momentum) and their squared values, helping the optimizer navigate the loss landscape more efficiently, especially when dealing with noisy or sparse gradients.

Adam is widely used because of its ability to achieve faster convergence than standard SGD and because it performs well on a variety of tasks. The update rule for Adam includes two parameters, **beta1** and **beta2**, which control the decay rates for the first and second moments of the gradients.

$$m_t = \beta_1 m_{t-1} + (1 - \beta_1)\nabla J(\theta)$$

$$v_t = \beta_2 v_{t-1} + (1 - \beta_2)(\nabla J(\theta))^2$$

$$\theta = \theta - \eta \cdot \frac{m_t}{\sqrt{v_t} + \epsilon}$$

Where:

- m_t and v_t are the first and second moment estimates, respectively.
- ϵ is a small constant to prevent division by zero.

Now, what to choose between SGD and Adam? Both optimizers have their advantages:

- **SGD** with momentum is often preferred for large-scale, high-dimensional datasets and is known to generalize better when fine-tuned.
- **Adam** is often chosen for its faster convergence and is a popular choice when training deep neural networks with complex architectures, especially when time is a constraint.

For most tasks, **Adam** is a good starting point due to its adaptive nature, but **SGD** (often with momentum) remains highly effective, especially in tasks like image classification or natural language processing where generalization is key.

Learning Rate Scheduling

The **learning rate** is one of the most important hyperparameters in training a neural network. A static learning rate can often cause issues. For instance, if the learning rate is too high, the model may never converge, bouncing around the optimal solution. If it's too low, the model may converge very slowly or get stuck in a suboptimal local minimum. To handle this, **learning rate scheduling** is used to adjust the learning rate dynamically during training.

In PyTorch, **learning rate schedulers** can adjust the learning rate based on the number of epochs or the performance of the model.

Common types of schedulers include:

- **StepLR**: Reduces the learning rate by a factor after a fixed number of epochs.
- **ExponentialLR**: Decays the learning rate by a fixed factor after every epoch.
- **ReduceLROnPlateau**: Reduces the learning rate when a monitored metric has stopped improving.

Implementing Optimizers and Learning Rate Scheduling

We will now implement **Adam** as our optimizer and use a **StepLR** scheduler to dynamically adjust the learning rate during training.

```
import torch.optim as optim

from torch.optim.lr_scheduler import StepLR


# Define the model, loss function, and optimizer
(assuming FishNet model from previous chapter)

model = FishNet(input_size, hidden_size, output_size)

criterion = torch.nn.MSELoss()  # Loss function for
regression

optimizer = optim.Adam(model.parameters(), lr=0.001)  #
Adam optimizer with an initial learning rate of 0.001


# Define a learning rate scheduler that reduces the
learning rate by a factor of 0.1 every 30 epochs

scheduler = StepLR(optimizer, step_size=30, gamma=0.1)
```

Here, in the above code,

- We initialize the **Adam optimizer** with a learning rate of 0.001.
- We use **StepLR** as our learning rate scheduler, which will reduce the learning rate by a factor of 0.1 every 30 epochs.

Neural Network Training with Dynamic Learning Rate Adjustment

We will integrate the optimizer and learning rate scheduler into the training loop.

```
# Training loop with learning rate scheduling
```

```
num_epochs = 100

for epoch in range(num_epochs):
    model.train()  # Set the model to training mode
    optimizer.zero_grad()  # Clear the previous gradients

    # Forward pass: Generate predictions
    outputs = model(X_train_tensor)

    # Compute the loss
    loss = criterion(outputs, y_train_tensor.unsqueeze(1))
# Ensure the target has the correct shape

    # Backward pass: Compute gradients
    loss.backward()

    # Update weights using Adam optimizer
    optimizer.step()

    # Adjust the learning rate using the scheduler
    scheduler.step()
```

```
    # Print the learning rate and loss every 10 epochs
    if (epoch + 1) % 10 == 0:
        current_lr = scheduler.get_last_lr()[0]  # Get the current learning rate
        print(f'Epoch [{epoch+1}/{num_epochs}], Loss: {loss.item():.4f}, Learning Rate: {current_lr:.6f}')
```

In this training loop,

- The **Adam optimizer** updates the weights based on the gradients.
- The **scheduler** dynamically adjusts the learning rate after every epoch using **`scheduler.step()`**. In this case, the learning rate is reduced by a factor of 0.1 every 30 epochs.
- The current learning rate is printed every 10 epochs to track how it changes over time.

Evaluating Trained Model

During the early stages of training, when the model is far from the optimal solution, a higher learning rate allows for faster exploration of the parameter space. As training progresses and the model approaches the optimal solution, lowering the learning rate helps fine-tune the weights more precisely without overshooting the minima.

After the training process is complete, we can evaluate the model on the test data, similar to how we did earlier.

```
# Set the model to evaluation mode
model.eval()


with torch.no_grad():  # Disable gradient computation
    test_outputs = model(X_test_tensor)
    test_loss = criterion(test_outputs, y_test_tensor.unsqueeze(1))
```

```
print(f'Test Loss: {test_loss.item():.4f}')
```

The test loss gives an indication of how well the model has generalized to unseen data, and the learning rate adjustments during training should have contributed to improved performance.

Gradient Computations with CUDA 12

Understanding Gradient Computation

In the training of neural networks, **gradient computation** plays a central role. Gradients are used during **backpropagation**, which is the process of calculating the partial derivatives of the loss function with respect to each of the model's parameters (weights and biases). These gradients tell the optimizer how to adjust the weights to minimize the loss. Without gradient computation, the model would have no way of learning from the data.

The **autograd** feature in PyTorch automates the process of computing these gradients. Each operation on tensors is tracked by PyTorch, and when **loss.backward()** is called, the framework uses the **chain rule** to compute the gradients of the loss with respect to each parameter in the model. This means that every tensor operation results in a computational graph, which is used to efficiently compute gradients.

Gradient Computations and GPUs

When working with small datasets or simple models, gradient computation on a CPU is often sufficient. However, for larger datasets and complex models with millions or even billions of parameters, CPU computation can be slow and inefficient. This is where **GPUs** (Graphics Processing Units) come in. GPUs are designed to handle parallel computations, which makes them ideal for the matrix operations involved in deep learning, especially for computing gradients.

By leveraging CUDA, PyTorch can offload the gradient computations to the GPU, significantly accelerating the training process, especially for large-scale models. CUDA-enabled GPUs can perform tensor operations in parallel across thousands of cores, which leads to faster gradient computations compared to CPUs. When using PyTorch, enabling **CUDA acceleration** is simple. By moving your model and data to the GPU, PyTorch automatically takes advantage of CUDA for faster computations.

CUDA Benefits for Gradient Computation

- **Parallelization**: GPUs can perform multiple computations simultaneously, making them faster than CPUs for tasks like gradient computation, which involves large matrix operations.
- **Scalability**: As the size of the dataset or the complexity of the model increases, CUDA

ensures that the operations remain efficient by distributing the workload across hundreds or thousands of GPU cores.
- **Efficiency in Large Models**: When training large neural networks with multiple layers and millions of parameters, the gradient calculations can be computationally expensive. Using CUDA accelerates this process, allowing for faster training and iteration.

Implementing Gradient Computation with CUDA 12

We will now demonstrate how to utilize **`CUDA 12`** to accelerate gradient computations for our neural network trained on the **`Fish Dataset`**. The steps include moving the model and data to the GPU, performing forward and backward passes on the GPU, and observing the performance gains.

Checking CUDA Availability

Before using CUDA, we need to check whether a CUDA-enabled GPU is available. PyTorch provides an easy way to do this with **`torch.cuda.is_available()`**.

```
# Check if CUDA is available

device = torch.device("cuda" if torch.cuda.is_available()
else "cpu")

print(f"Using device: {device}")
```

If a GPU is available, this command will return **`"cuda"`**, indicating that all computations will be performed on the GPU. If no GPU is available, it will return **`"cpu"`**.

Moving Model and Data to GPU

Once CUDA is available, the next step is to move both the model and the data to the GPU. In PyTorch, tensors and models must be explicitly moved to the GPU using the **`.to(device)`** method. We will modify the model and data to ensure they are processed on the GPU.

```
# Move the model to the GPU

model = FishNet(input_size, hidden_size,
output_size).to(device)



# Move the data to the GPU
```

```
X_train_tensor = X_train_tensor.to(device)

y_train_tensor = y_train_tensor.to(device)

X_test_tensor = X_test_tensor.to(device)

y_test_tensor = y_test_tensor.to(device)
```

As per the above script, both the model and the data are moved to the GPU using **`.to(device)`**. This ensures that all forward and backward computations are performed on the GPU.

Training Model with CUDA-Accelerated Gradient Computations

Now that the model and data are on the GPU, we can proceed with training. PyTorch will automatically handle the gradient computations on the GPU once everything is moved to the CUDA device.

```
# Define the loss function and optimizer (now on the GPU)

criterion = torch.nn.MSELoss()  # Loss function for
regression

optimizer = torch.optim.Adam(model.parameters(),
lr=0.001)  # Adam optimizer


# Training loop

num_epochs = 100


for epoch in range(num_epochs):

   model.train()  # Set the model to training mode

   optimizer.zero_grad()  # Clear the previous gradients
```

```
    # Forward pass: Generate predictions (now on GPU)
    outputs = model(X_train_tensor)

    # Compute the loss (now on GPU)
    loss = criterion(outputs, y_train_tensor.unsqueeze(1))

    # Backward pass: Compute gradients (now on GPU)
    loss.backward()

    # Update weights
    optimizer.step()

    # Print loss every 10 epochs
    if (epoch + 1) % 10 == 0:
        print(f'Epoch [{epoch+1}/{num_epochs}], Loss:
{loss.item():.4f}')
```

In this training loop:

- The forward pass, loss computation, backward pass (gradient computation), and weight updates are all performed on the GPU.
- The **loss.backward()** function computes the gradients for each parameter with respect to the loss using CUDA-enabled gradient computations.

Evaluating Model on GPU

After training, we can evaluate the model's performance on the test set, also using the GPU.

```
# Set the model to evaluation mode
model.eval()


# Disable gradient computation during evaluation
with torch.no_grad():
    # Forward pass on the test data (now on GPU)
    test_outputs = model(X_test_tensor)


    # Compute the test loss (now on GPU)
    test_loss = criterion(test_outputs,
y_test_tensor.unsqueeze(1))


    print(f'Test Loss: {test_loss.item():.4f}')
```

By moving the evaluation step to the GPU as well, all computations, including the forward pass and loss calculation, are accelerated.

Measuring GPU Performance

To observe the benefits of using CUDA, you can measure the training time on both the CPU and GPU for comparison. Following is how we use PyTorch's **`time`** module to check the duration of the training loop:

```
import time


# Measure time for training on GPU
start_time = time.time()
```

```
# Training loop
for epoch in range(num_epochs):
    model.train()
    optimizer.zero_grad()
    outputs = model(X_train_tensor)
    loss = criterion(outputs, y_train_tensor.unsqueeze(1))
    loss.backward()
    optimizer.step()

end_time = time.time()
print(f'Training time on GPU: {end_time - start_time:.2f}
seconds')
```

You can then compare this timing with the training time on the CPU to see how much faster the training is with CUDA acceleration.

By utilizing CUDA 12 for gradient computations, you can expect a significant reduction in the time required for training, especially when working with large datasets and deep models. The speedup comes from the parallel processing capabilities of GPUs, which handle matrix multiplications, convolutions, and gradient computations much more efficiently than CPUs. For tasks involving large amounts of data or highly complex models, the benefits of using CUDA become more apparent.

Mixed Precision Training with AMP

Understanding Automatic Mixed Precision

Automatic Mixed Precision (AMP) is an advanced feature that enables faster and more memory-efficient training by utilizing a mix of 16-bit (half precision) and 32-bit (single precision) floating-point arithmetic. Traditionally, deep learning models have been trained using 32-bit floating-point numbers, which provide sufficient precision but can be computationally expensive and require significant memory. **AMP** allows for switching between 16-bit and 32-bit precision during training, providing a way to reduce memory usage and improve the speed of operations, particularly on modern GPUs.

The key idea behind **`mixed precision training`** is that not all parts of the model need 32-bit precision. Operations like matrix multiplications, which are abundant in deep learning, can often be done in 16-bit precision without losing much accuracy. On the other hand, more sensitive calculations, such as the loss and gradients, can still be computed in 32-bit precision to ensure stability. This approach strikes a balance between computational efficiency and numerical precision.

Benefits of AMP

- **Speed Improvements**: Since 16-bit operations are faster than 32-bit operations on modern GPUs, mixed precision allows certain computations to be executed much more quickly, leading to a reduction in overall training time.
- **Reduced Memory Usage**: Using 16-bit floating-point numbers consumes less memory, allowing larger models or larger batches to fit into the GPU memory.
- **Minimal Loss of Accuracy**: The smart combination of 16-bit and 32-bit operations ensures that the model's accuracy is minimally impacted while still gaining performance improvements.

AMP automatically decides when to use 16-bit precision and when to use 32-bit precision. PyTorch manages this process using the **`GradScaler`**, which scales up the gradients when necessary to prevent **`underflow`** (a situation where gradients become too small to be represented in 16-bit). This scaling ensures that using 16-bit precision does not lead to instability in training.

Implementing AMP

We will now demonstrate how to implement **AMP**. We will use PyTorch's **`torch.cuda.amp`** package to enable mixed precision and compare its performance with full 32-bit precision training.

Initializing AMP Components

To enable AMP, we need to modify the training loop slightly by using the **`autocast()`** context manager, which enables mixed precision, and the **`GradScaler`**, which scales the gradients to ensure stability during backpropagation.

```
from torch.cuda.amp import autocast, GradScaler
```

```
# Initialize the GradScaler

scaler = GradScaler()


# Model, loss function, and optimizer (moved to GPU)

model = FishNet(input_size, hidden_size,
output_size).to(device)

criterion = torch.nn.MSELoss()  # Loss function for
regression

optimizer = torch.optim.Adam(model.parameters(),
lr=0.001)  # Adam optimizer
```

In this setup,

- The **GradScaler** scales the loss and gradients to avoid underflow issues that may arise when using 16-bit precision.
- We will use **`autocast()`**, which enables mixed precision for operations that are safe to compute with 16-bit precision.

Training Loop with AMP

We will modify the training loop to incorporate mixed precision. The primary difference here is the use of **`autocast()`** during the forward pass and the use of **`scaler`** for backward propagation and optimization.

```
# Training loop with mixed precision

num_epochs = 100


for epoch in range(num_epochs):

   model.train()  # Set the model to training mode

   optimizer.zero_grad()  # Clear the previous gradients
```

```
    # Enable automatic mixed precision for forward pass
    with autocast():
        # Forward pass: Generate predictions (now in mixed
precision)
        outputs = model(X_train_tensor)

        # Compute the loss (in mixed precision)
        loss = criterion(outputs,
y_train_tensor.unsqueeze(1))

    # Backward pass with gradient scaling
    scaler.scale(loss).backward()

    # Step the optimizer using the scaled gradients
    scaler.step(optimizer)

    # Update the scale for next iteration
    scaler.update()

    # Print loss every 10 epochs
    if (epoch + 1) % 10 == 0:
```

```
        print(f'Epoch [{epoch+1}/{num_epochs}], Loss:
{loss.item():.4f}')
```

Here,

- The **autocast()** context ensures that operations inside it are executed in mixed precision, where appropriate.
- The **GradScaler** scales the loss and gradients during the backward pass to ensure the precision of small gradient values is not lost when using 16-bit floats.
- The optimizer step and gradient update are performed through **scaler.step()**, ensuring that the scaled gradients are used for updating the model's parameters.

Comparing Memory Usage and Speed

Now, to highlight the benefits of mixed precision training, you can measure both the **training time** and **memory usage** on the GPU for both standard 32-bit and mixed precision training.

```
import torch

import time



# Timing and memory measurement functions

def measure_performance(model, X_train_tensor,
y_train_tensor, use_amp=False):

   start_time = time.time()

   model.train()



   # Optimizer and scaler setup

   optimizer = torch.optim.Adam(model.parameters(),
lr=0.001)

   criterion = torch.nn.MSELoss()
```

```
    scaler = GradScaler() if use_amp else None

    for epoch in range(10):  # Shorter training for
comparison
        optimizer.zero_grad()

        # Use mixed precision if enabled
        if use_amp:
            with autocast():
                outputs = model(X_train_tensor)
                loss = criterion(outputs,
y_train_tensor.unsqueeze(1))
        else:
            outputs = model(X_train_tensor)
            loss = criterion(outputs,
y_train_tensor.unsqueeze(1))

        # Backward pass
        if use_amp:
            scaler.scale(loss).backward()
            scaler.step(optimizer)
            scaler.update()
```

```
        else:
            loss.backward()
            optimizer.step()

    end_time = time.time()
    print(f"Training time with {'AMP' if use_amp else 'FP32'}: {end_time - start_time:.4f} seconds")

# Measure performance with and without AMP
measure_performance(model, X_train_tensor, y_train_tensor, use_amp=False)  # Full 32-bit precision
measure_performance(model, X_train_tensor, y_train_tensor, use_amp=True)   # Mixed precision
```

Here, we define a function to train the model either with full 32-bit precision or with **AMP** enabled and measure the total training time. You can compare the two results to see how much faster mixed precision training is compared to 32-bit precision.

Results of Mixed Precision Training

With AMP, you should observe:

- **Speed Improvements**: The total training time with AMP is generally faster compared to full 32-bit training due to the use of 16-bit precision for certain operations, especially on modern GPUs.
- **Memory Savings**: The reduced precision for most operations also reduces memory consumption, which can allow for larger batch sizes or deeper models to be trained on the same hardware.

The main advantage of mixed precision training is that it offers these performance gains without sacrificing accuracy, as critical operations (like gradient calculations and loss functions) remain in 32-bit precision.

Using torch.profiler for Training Insights

Understanding torch.profiler

`torch.profiler` is a powerful tool provided by PyTorch that helps analyze the performance of neural network training by identifying bottlenecks in various parts of the model. This profiler can monitor and record the performance of different operations, such as matrix multiplications, gradient computations, and data transfers between the CPU and GPU. With this analysis, developers can gain insight into which parts of their code might be slowing down the training process and take steps to optimize those areas.

In large-scale deep learning models, especially when using GPUs or distributed training, understanding where inefficiencies lie becomes crucial to improving performance. The **`torch.profiler`** is particularly useful for:

- **Identifying slow operations** that take up too much computation time.
- Measuring data transfer times between the CPU and GPU.
- **Profiling GPU utilization**, allowing you to detect if the GPU is being underutilized.
- **Optimizing bottlenecks** in model training, which can lead to faster training times and more efficient resource usage.

`torch.profiler` collects detailed information about the time spent in each operation, both on the CPU and GPU. You can configure the profiler to track specific types of events, such as operations or memory usage, and generate detailed reports. This tool is highly customizable and allows you to analyze different components of the training process.

Setting up torch.profiler

We will now demonstrate how to use **`torch.profiler`** to analyze the training process of our **`FishNet`** model. First, we need to import the necessary modules and set up the profiler.

```
import torch.profiler



# Define the profiling activity

activities = [

    torch.profiler.ProfilerActivity.CPU,

    torch.profiler.ProfilerActivity.CUDA
```

```
]
```

In the above code, we specify that we want to profile both **CPU** and **GPU** (CUDA) activities. This ensures that the profiler collects performance data from both the CPU and the GPU during training.

Profiling Training Loop

We will now integrate **`torch.profiler`** into our training loop to collect detailed information about the operations performed during each epoch.

```
# Initialize the profiler with specific activities

with torch.profiler.profile(activities=activities,
record_shapes=True, profile_memory=True, with_stack=True)
as profiler:

   model.train()  # Set the model to training mode

   optimizer.zero_grad()  # Clear the previous gradients


   # Forward pass: Generate predictions

   outputs = model(X_train_tensor)


   # Compute the loss

   loss = criterion(outputs, y_train_tensor.unsqueeze(1))


   # Backward pass: Compute gradients

   loss.backward()
```

```
    # Update weights

    optimizer.step()


    # Record the profiler data after the forward and
backward passes

    profiler.step()
```

In the above, following are the key elements:

- **record_shapes=True**: This records the shapes of the input and output tensors, which can help you identify inefficiencies related to tensor sizes.
- **profile_memory=True**: This records memory usage, allowing you to identify memory bottlenecks during training.
- **with_stack=True**: This captures the stack trace for each operation, providing additional context for profiling data.

The **profiler.step()** call records data for each training step. You can insert this at different points in the training loop to capture detailed insights for specific operations.

Generating Report

Once the profiling data is collected, you can export the results to view a detailed report of the operations and their time consumption.

```
# Print profiling results to the console

print(profiler.key_averages().table(sort_by="cpu_time_tot
al", row_limit=10))
```

This prints a table summarizing the operations with the highest **CPU** time usage, sorted by total CPU time. You can adjust the **sort_by** parameter to view different performance metrics, such as **cuda_time_total** to focus on GPU time.

For more detailed analysis, you can also export the profiling data to **TensorBoard** for visualization.

```
# Export profiling data to a TensorBoard file
```

```
with torch.profiler.profile(
    activities=activities,
    record_shapes=True,

on_trace_ready=torch.profiler.tensorboard_trace_handler('
./log')) as profiler:

    for epoch in range(num_epochs):
        # Training loop code
        outputs = model(X_train_tensor)
        loss = criterion(outputs,
y_train_tensor.unsqueeze(1))
        loss.backward()
        optimizer.step()

        # Step the profiler to record data for this
iteration
        profiler.step()

print("Profiler data saved for TensorBoard
visualization.")
```

Visualizing Profiler Data in TensorBoard

To gain more insights into the performance bottlenecks, we can visualize the profiling data using

TensorBoard. TensorBoard provides a graphical interface that allows you to easily inspect the performance of each layer, operation, or data transfer step.

To view the profiler data, launch TensorBoard with the following command:

```
tensorboard --logdir=./log
```

Once TensorBoard is running, you can navigate to the **Profile** tab to see detailed visualizations of the training bottlenecks. These visualizations show the timeline of each operation, the amount of time spent in different layers, and GPU utilization.

Analyzing Training Bottlenecks

With **torch.profiler** integrated into the training loop, you can now analyze the collected data to identify the key bottlenecks. Some common areas where bottlenecks might arise include:

- **Matrix Operations**: Operations like matrix multiplications or convolutions might take too long, indicating that optimizations in how the tensors are handled (e.g., batching, using mixed precision) might be needed.
- **Data Transfers**: If data transfer between the CPU and GPU is slow, it could mean that operations are not being efficiently parallelized, or too much data is being transferred between the two.
- **GPU Underutilization**: If the GPU is not being fully utilized, the profiler might show long gaps where the GPU is idle. This could be due to inefficient code or long-running CPU operations that are blocking GPU execution.

Optimizing Training Process

Once you have identified the bottlenecks using **torch.profiler**, the next step is to optimize the training loop. Some potential optimizations include:

- **Batch Size Adjustment**: Increasing the batch size can help better utilize the GPU and reduce idle times.
- **Mixed Precision Training**: Using AMP (Automatic Mixed Precision) can speed up training and reduce memory usage, which might alleviate some bottlenecks related to memory or computational overload.
- **DataLoader Optimization**: If data loading is slow, consider using **num_workers** in the **DataLoader** to load data in parallel, which can improve training speed by reducing data-fetching times.

This whole profiling tool is essential for optimizing large models or long-running training jobs, and when combined with visual tools like TensorBoard, it provides a clear path to making targeted improvements in your deep learning pipeline.

Summary

In this chapter, the focus was on training neural networks using PyTorch, with a deep dive into various components and techniques that improve the efficiency and performance of the training process. The chapter started with an explanation of the general training workflow, covering the essential steps of forward passes, backward passes, and weight updates. Different optimization algorithms were then introduced, with emphasis on **`Adam`** and **`SGD`**, showing how they adjust the learning rate dynamically using learning rate schedulers like **`StepLR`**.

Following this, the role of **`gradient computations`** was explored, and it was demonstrated how leveraging **`CUDA 12`** for GPU-based computation significantly improves the speed of training by parallelizing operations. The concept of **`AMP`** was introduced next, explaining how AMP accelerates training by using a combination of 16-bit and 32-bit floating-point numbers, reducing memory usage without sacrificing accuracy.

Finally, the chapter explored the use of **`torch.profiler`** to analyze training bottlenecks. By profiling both CPU and GPU activities, it became possible to identify inefficiencies in the training process, providing a way to optimize operations, improve memory usage, and accelerate training. The overall focus of this chapter was on providing practical tools and techniques to enhance training performance, making neural networks faster and more resource-efficient.

CHAPTER 5: ADVANCED NEURAL NETWORK ARCHITECTURES

Overview

In this chapter, we will explore **advanced neural network architectures** in PyTorch, focusing on building custom layers and leveraging powerful modern techniques. We will start by learning how to create **custom layers in PyTorch**, which allows developers to go beyond the built-in layers and design their own operations, giving more control and flexibility in shaping the architecture of neural networks. This is especially useful when working on specialized tasks or novel architectures that require more tailored layers.

Next, we will dive into **transformers**, one of the most influential innovations in neural network design. Transformers are now at the core of many cutting-edge models, particularly in NLP and other sequence-related tasks. We will explore how transformers operate, particularly focusing on attention mechanisms and their ability to model relationships in sequential data more efficiently than traditional architectures like RNNs.

Finally, we will learn about **torch.compile()** for achieving **high-performance training**. This feature allows you to optimize your PyTorch code for better performance, particularly with large models, by compiling and optimizing the computation graph, ensuring that training is faster and more efficient.

Building Custom Layers

Custom layers in neural networks provide a way to go beyond the built-in layers offered by PyTorch to create operations that are tailored to specific needs. While PyTorch offers a rich set of standard layers, such as fully connected layers, convolutional layers, and recurrent layers, there are many scenarios where custom functionality is needed. For example, when working on specialized tasks like scientific computing, signal processing, or novel research areas, the available layers might not capture the unique requirements of the model. Designing custom layers also allows for more control over how data is transformed as it moves through the network, providing a path to optimize performance or adapt to specific input types.

In practice, building custom layers is particularly helpful when the model needs to incorporate new operations that PyTorch doesn't natively support. Researchers often develop custom layers to experiment with novel architectures or apply neural networks to tasks that require unique mathematical transformations. Furthermore, custom layers are a powerful tool when creating highly specialized models for industrial applications or research, where fine-tuned control over how the data flows through the network can lead to significant performance improvements.

PyTorch makes creating custom layers simple by allowing you to subclass **nn.Module** and define your operations in the **forward()** method. This flexibility enables the construction of any operation, from basic linear layers with custom weight initializations to entirely new layer types that involve complex, non-standard mathematical transformations.

Design Custom Layers

To design a custom layer, we will start by subclassing **nn.Module**. We will implement a simple example to demonstrate how this works, where we will create a custom layer that applies a non-standard mathematical transformation to the input.

```
import torch

import torch.nn as nn


# Define a custom layer that applies a non-standard
mathematical operation

class CustomLayer(nn.Module):

   def __init__(self, input_size, output_size):

       super(CustomLayer, self).__init__()

       # Define a learnable parameter (weights)

       self.weights =
nn.Parameter(torch.randn(input_size, output_size))


       # Define a bias term

       self.bias = nn.Parameter(torch.randn(output_size))


   def forward(self, x):

       # Custom forward pass

       # This applies a matrix multiplication followed by
an element-wise exponential operation
```

```
        x = torch.mm(x, self.weights) + self.bias

        return torch.exp(x)  # Apply an element-wise
exponential function


# Test the custom layer with random input

input_tensor = torch.randn(3, 5)  # A batch of 3 samples
with 5 features each

custom_layer = CustomLayer(input_size=5, output_size=4)

output_tensor = custom_layer(input_tensor)


print(output_tensor)
```

In the above script,

- **__init__()**: In the constructor, we define the learnable parameters. Here, we create a weight matrix and a bias vector, both of which are registered as **nn.Parameter**, allowing PyTorch to track them during the training process.
- **forward()**: The forward method defines the transformation applied to the input data. In this example, we use matrix multiplication (**torch.mm**) to apply a linear transformation, then add the bias term, and finally apply an element-wise exponential function to the result.

This custom layer can now be integrated into any PyTorch model, just like any other layer.

Integrating Custom Layers into Neural Network

We can now incorporate this custom layer into our existing **FishNet** model. We will replace one of the standard layers with our newly designed custom layer.

```
# Define a modified version of the FishNet model that
uses the custom layer

class CustomFishNet(nn.Module):
```

```
    def __init__(self, input_size, hidden_size,
output_size):
        super(CustomFishNet, self).__init__()
        # Use the custom layer instead of a standard
linear layer
        self.custom_layer = CustomLayer(input_size,
hidden_size)
        self.fc1 = nn.Linear(hidden_size, hidden_size)  #
Fully connected layer
        self.fc2 = nn.Linear(hidden_size, output_size)  #
Output layer
        self.relu = nn.ReLU()  # Activation function

    def forward(self, x):
        # Forward pass through custom layer and other
layers
        x = self.custom_layer(x)
        x = self.relu(self.fc1(x))
        x = self.fc2(x)
        return x

# Initialize the model with the custom layer
model = CustomFishNet(input_size=5, hidden_size=10,
output_size=1)
```

```
# Test the model with random input

test_input = torch.randn(3, 5)  # A batch of 3 samples
with 5 features each

output = model(test_input)

print(output)
```

Here, we replaced the first standard fully connected layer with the **CustomLayer**. This allows us to incorporate non-standard mathematical transformations into the network. The remaining layers follow the usual architecture, with fully connected layers and an activation function (ReLU).

Training Model with Custom Layers

Once the custom layer is integrated into the model, the training process remains the same as with standard layers. The optimizer and loss function will handle the custom layer's parameters automatically, just like any other layer in PyTorch.

```
# Define the loss function and optimizer

criterion = nn.MSELoss()

optimizer = torch.optim.Adam(model.parameters(),
lr=0.001)


# Dummy training loop

num_epochs = 100

for epoch in range(num_epochs):

   model.train()

   optimizer.zero_grad()
```

```
    # Forward pass
    outputs = model(X_train_tensor)
    loss = criterion(outputs, y_train_tensor.unsqueeze(1))

    # Backward pass and optimization
    loss.backward()
    optimizer.step()

    if (epoch + 1) % 10 == 0:
        print(f'Epoch [{epoch+1}/{num_epochs}], Loss:
{loss.item():.4f}')
```

By following the standard training procedure, PyTorch will compute gradients for the custom layer's parameters during the backward pass and update them accordingly. The custom layer is fully integrated into the autograd mechanism, meaning that its parameters will automatically be adjusted during training.

Up and Running with Transformers

Transformers have revolutionized the field of deep learning, especially in NLP tasks, and they continue to push the boundaries of what neural networks can achieve. Introduced in the landmark paper "Attention Is All You Need" by Vaswani et al. (2017), transformers are distinct from traditional architectures like RNNs and CNNs. While RNNs and CNNs are well-suited to specific tasks, transformers have emerged as the go-to architecture for sequence-based problems, thanks to their ability to capture long-range dependencies in data through a mechanism called **self-attention**.

Unlike RNNs, which process sequential data step by step and are limited by their sequential nature, transformers handle entire sequences in parallel. This parallelism allows transformers to be much more efficient and scalable when dealing with large datasets. Similarly, while CNNs excel at local feature detection through convolutions, they are less adept at capturing global relationships between data points, particularly in tasks like language modeling. In contrast, transformers use

self-attention to model relationships between any two elements in a sequence, irrespective of their distance from each other.

Transformers vs RNNs and CNNs

RNNs are designed for sequential data, such as time-series data or text. They process data one step at a time, which makes them inherently slow for long sequences. Additionally, RNNs struggle to capture long-term dependencies due to issues like **vanishing gradients**. Even with advanced variants like LSTM networks and Gated Recurrent Units (GRUs), these architectures still face limitations when handling very long sequences. CNNs excel at extracting local features from data, particularly in tasks involving images. By applying filters, CNNs detect patterns like edges and textures, making them highly effective for computer vision. However, CNNs are not designed to handle long-range dependencies, especially in sequential data, as their receptive fields are limited.

Transformers, on the other hand, use **self-attention** to capture dependencies between elements in a sequence, regardless of their position. The self-attention mechanism enables the model to focus on relevant parts of the input when making predictions. Because of this, transformers can capture both local and global dependencies efficiently. Their ability to process data in parallel also makes them highly scalable, a key advantage over RNNs.

The **self-attention mechanism** is at the heart of what makes transformers powerful. In self-attention, each element in the input sequence is compared with every other element to calculate attention scores. These scores determine how much attention the model should pay to other elements when making predictions. This ability to selectively focus on different parts of the input is what allows transformers to capture complex dependencies in data.

Sample Program: Building Transformer-based Architectures

Transformers have had a profound impact on fields like NLP, machine translation, and even computer vision. One of the most well-known transformer models is **BERT (Bidirectional Encoder Representations from Transformers)**, which demonstrated the power of pre-trained language models and brought significant improvements to various NLP tasks, including question answering and text classification. In recent years, transformer-based architectures have been extended to other domains as well, such as speech recognition and protein folding.

Now, we will gain practical experience with transformer architectures in PyTorch. PyTorch provides the **torch.nn.Transformer** class, which offers a modular implementation of the transformer model. We will define a simple transformer model using PyTorch's built-in classes. This model will contain an encoder-decoder architecture that can process sequence data efficiently.

```
import torch
```

```
import torch.nn as nn

import torch.optim as optim

from torch.nn import Transformer


class SimpleTransformerModel(nn.Module):

   def __init__(self, input_size, output_size, nhead,
num_encoder_layers, num_decoder_layers, dim_feedforward):

       super(SimpleTransformerModel, self).__init__()


       # Define the transformer module

       self.transformer = Transformer(

           d_model=input_size,  # Dimension of the input
and output embeddings

           nhead=nhead,  # Number of heads in the multi-
head attention mechanism

           num_encoder_layers=num_encoder_layers,  #
Number of encoder layers

           num_decoder_layers=num_decoder_layers,  #
Number of decoder layers

           dim_feedforward=dim_feedforward  # Dimension
of the feedforward layers

       )
```

```
        # Embedding layers for input and output sequences
        self.input_embedding = nn.Linear(input_size,
input_size)
        self.output_embedding = nn.Linear(output_size,
output_size)

        # Final linear layer for prediction
        self.fc_out = nn.Linear(input_size, output_size)

    def forward(self, src, tgt):
        # Pass the input and output sequences through the
embedding layers
        src_embedded = self.input_embedding(src)
        tgt_embedded = self.output_embedding(tgt)

        # Forward pass through the transformer
        transformer_output =
self.transformer(src_embedded, tgt_embedded)

        # Final output layer
        output = self.fc_out(transformer_output)
        return output
```

The transformer components includes:

- **Multi-Head Attention**: Transformers use **multi-head attention**, where the input sequence is processed in parallel across multiple attention heads. Each head learns to focus on different parts of the sequence, allowing the model to capture multiple types of relationships in the data. In the model, this is represented by the **`nhead`** parameter, which controls how many attention heads are used.
- **Positional Encoding**: Since transformers do not inherently understand the order of sequences (unlike RNNs, which process data sequentially), they rely on **positional encodings** to introduce information about the relative position of elements in a sequence. PyTorch's **`torch.nn.Transformer`** handles this internally by adding position embeddings to the input sequences.
- **Encoder-Decoder Architecture**: The model consists of an **encoder** that processes the input sequence and a **decoder** that generates the output sequence based on the encoded input. Each encoder and decoder block is composed of layers of self-attention and feedforward networks. The **`num_encoder_layers`** and **`num_decoder_layers`** parameters determine the depth of these components.
- **Feedforward Layers**: After attention has been applied, the data is passed through fully connected feedforward layers, which apply additional transformations. The **`dim_feedforward`** parameter controls the size of the hidden layer in these feedforward networks.

Training Transformer Model

We will now integrate this above transformer model into a training loop and train the model to predict sequential data.

```
# Define the model parameters

input_size = 10

output_size = 10

nhead = 2

num_encoder_layers = 2

num_decoder_layers = 2

dim_feedforward = 512
```

```
# Initialize the model

model = SimpleTransformerModel(input_size, output_size,
nhead, num_encoder_layers, num_decoder_layers,
dim_feedforward)


# Define the loss function and optimizer

criterion = nn.MSELoss()

optimizer = optim.Adam(model.parameters(), lr=0.001)


# Example of source and target sequences (random data for
illustration)

src_sequence = torch.rand(5, 3, input_size)  # Sequence
length of 5, batch size of 3

tgt_sequence = torch.rand(5, 3, output_size)  # Sequence
length of 5, batch size of 3


# Training loop

num_epochs = 50

for epoch in range(num_epochs):

   model.train()

   optimizer.zero_grad()


   # Forward pass
```

```
    output = model(src_sequence, tgt_sequence)


    # Compute the loss

    loss = criterion(output, tgt_sequence)


    # Backward pass and optimization

    loss.backward()

    optimizer.step()


    if (epoch + 1) % 10 == 0:

        print(f'Epoch [{epoch+1}/{num_epochs}], Loss:
{loss.item():.4f}')
```

In this example, the transformer model processes a sequence of input data and generates a corresponding output sequence. The model learns by minimizing the loss between the predicted output sequence and the target sequence. While this is a simple demonstration, transformers are capable of handling much more complex tasks, especially in areas like language modeling, machine translation, and even image generation.

One of the strengths of transformer-based architectures is their scalability and flexibility. The number of layers, attention heads, and feedforward dimensions can be adjusted to fit the complexity of the task. This flexibility, combined with their parallelization capabilities, allows transformers to outperform traditional architectures on a wide range of tasks. In tasks like **language translation**, models like **GPT**, **BERT**, and **T5** have set new performance benchmarks by understanding context in a deep and nuanced way. They have also been successfully applied to **time series forecasting**, **speech recognition**, and even **image processing**, demonstrating their versatility. By focusing on the relationships between data points, transformers have opened up new possibilities in how we approach complex learning problems.

torch.compile() for High-Performance Training

`torch.compile()` is a new feature introduced in PyTorch 2.0 aimed at improving the performance of neural networks by optimizing the computational graph. This function compiles your PyTorch model into a more efficient form by applying optimizations that reduce overhead and speed up training and inference. Prior to the introduction of **`torch.compile()`**, PyTorch operated in an eager execution mode, which allowed for dynamic execution and flexibility, but at the cost of performance. With **`torch.compile()`**, PyTorch now offers an optional mode that brings significant speed improvements while retaining the dynamic nature PyTorch users value.

The key benefit of **`torch.compile()`** lies in its ability to automatically optimize models for **`high-performance training`**, without requiring any changes to the underlying code. It wraps the model in a compiler, applying optimizations such as **`fusion of operations`**, **`eliminating redundancies`**, and **`improving memory efficiency`**. This results in faster execution times, especially for large-scale models or complex architectures like transformers and custom layers.

We will now demonstrate how to use **`torch.compile()`** to optimize our neural network architecture, including the custom layers and transformer model we've built so far.

torch.compile() Use-cases

- **Large Transformer Models**: Models like **BERT** and **GPT**, which involve heavy matrix operations and attention mechanisms, benefit significantly from **`torch.compile()`** due to the optimizations in handling large-scale tensor computations.
- **Custom Architectures**: In research settings, where custom layers or operations are developed, **`torch.compile()`** can optimize these layers without requiring manual intervention. This reduces the need for hand-tuning and allows researchers to focus on the architecture itself.
- **Time-Critical Applications**: In industries where time is of the essence, such as autonomous driving or real-time recommendation systems, reducing training or inference times through **`torch.compile()`** can make a tangible impact on the performance of deployed systems.

Implementing torch.compile() in PyTorch

The process of applying **`torch.compile()`** to a model is simple and involves just one additional line of code. We will use it to optimize the **`SimpleTransformerModel`** we created in the previous section.

```
import torch
```

```
import torch.nn as nn
from torch.optim import Adam
from torch.nn import Transformer
import torch.compile  # Import torch.compile (available in PyTorch 2.0+)

# Define the transformer model (already defined in the previous section)
class SimpleTransformerModel(nn.Module):
   def __init__(self, input_size, output_size, nhead, num_encoder_layers, num_decoder_layers, dim_feedforward):
       super(SimpleTransformerModel, self).__init__()

       self.transformer = Transformer(
           d_model=input_size,
           nhead=nhead,
           num_encoder_layers=num_encoder_layers,
           num_decoder_layers=num_decoder_layers,
           dim_feedforward=dim_feedforward
       )

       self.input_embedding = nn.Linear(input_size, input_size)
```

```
        self.output_embedding = nn.Linear(output_size,
output_size)
        self.fc_out = nn.Linear(input_size, output_size)

    def forward(self, src, tgt):
        src_embedded = self.input_embedding(src)
        tgt_embedded = self.output_embedding(tgt)
        transformer_output =
self.transformer(src_embedded, tgt_embedded)
        output = self.fc_out(transformer_output)
        return output

# Initialize the model with the same architecture
model = SimpleTransformerModel(input_size=10,
output_size=10, nhead=2, num_encoder_layers=2,
num_decoder_layers=2, dim_feedforward=512)

# Apply torch.compile() to optimize the model
compiled_model = torch.compile(model)

# Define loss function and optimizer
criterion = nn.MSELoss()
optimizer = Adam(compiled_model.parameters(), lr=0.001)
```

```
# Dummy data for training
src_sequence = torch.rand(5, 3, 10)  # Sequence length of 5, batch size of 3
tgt_sequence = torch.rand(5, 3, 10)

# Training loop with the compiled model
num_epochs = 50
for epoch in range(num_epochs):
    compiled_model.train()
    optimizer.zero_grad()

    # Forward pass using the compiled model
    output = compiled_model(src_sequence, tgt_sequence)

    # Compute the loss
    loss = criterion(output, tgt_sequence)

    # Backward pass and optimization
    loss.backward()
    optimizer.step()
```

```
    if (epoch + 1) % 10 == 0:
        print(f'Epoch [{epoch+1}/{num_epochs}], Loss:
{loss.item():.4f}')
```

Here, the call to **torch.compile(model)** wraps the model in a compilation framework that optimizes it for performance. This includes both the forward and backward passes of the training loop. Once compiled, the model runs faster, as redundant operations are eliminated, and operations are fused together where possible.

Comparing Performance

Now, to see the benefits of **torch.compile()** in action, you can compare the training speed and memory usage of the compiled model against the non-compiled model. Following is how we time the training loop for both cases.

```
import time


# Timing the non-compiled model
start_time = time.time()


# Train the non-compiled model
for epoch in range(num_epochs):
    model.train()
    optimizer.zero_grad()
    output = model(src_sequence, tgt_sequence)
    loss = criterion(output, tgt_sequence)
    loss.backward()
    optimizer.step()
```

```
end_time = time.time()
print(f"Training time without torch.compile: {end_time -
start_time:.2f} seconds")

# Timing the compiled model
start_time = time.time()

# Train the compiled model
for epoch in range(num_epochs):
    compiled_model.train()
    optimizer.zero_grad()
    output = compiled_model(src_sequence, tgt_sequence)
    loss = criterion(output, tgt_sequence)
    loss.backward()
    optimizer.step()

end_time = time.time()
print(f"Training time with torch.compile: {end_time -
start_time:.2f} seconds")
```

If we compare the two timing results, you can observe how much faster the training process is when using **torch.compile()**. For large models and datasets, the speed improvements can be substantial, especially when the model involves computationally expensive operations like multi-head attention or custom layers.

By introducing **torch.compile()**, PyTorch bridges the gap between the flexibility of eager execution and the performance benefits of static graph execution. This feature enables developers to optimize their models effortlessly, significantly improving training speed and memory efficiency. Whether you are working on transformer architectures, custom neural networks, or deep learning models for production environments, **torch.compile()** provides a straightforward solution to achieve high-performance training without altering the underlying architecture or code structure.

Summary

In this chapter, the exploration centered on advanced neural network architectures and practical implementations in PyTorch. Starting with the concept of custom layers, it was demonstrated how designing these layers allows for more flexibility in neural network structures, enabling the creation of unique transformations and operations beyond the built-in layers provided by PyTorch. The necessity for custom layers was linked to specialized tasks and research, where predefined layers are insufficient for solving complex problems.

Following this, the chapter moved to transformer architectures, focusing on how they differ from traditional RNNs and CNNs by utilizing self-attention mechanisms. This approach allows transformers to capture long-range dependencies in data more efficiently. The practical implementation of a transformer-based model illustrated the power of this architecture, particularly in handling sequential data tasks like language modeling and machine translation.

Finally, the use of **torch.compile()** was introduced as a method to optimize models for high-performance training. This feature in PyTorch 2.0 allows for faster training and reduced memory usage by compiling and optimizing the computation graph. By applying **torch.compile()** to advanced architectures like transformers, the chapter demonstrated how training speed and efficiency can be significantly improved without altering the model's architecture. These insights highlighted the critical role of optimization in deep learning projects, especially when handling large and complex models.

CHAPTER 6: QUANTIZATION AND MODEL OPTIMIZATION

Overview

In this chapter, the focus will be on **model quantization** and optimization techniques that are essential for improving the efficiency of neural networks, especially when deploying them in production environments. Quantization refers to the process of reducing the precision of the model's weights and activations, typically from 32-bit floating-point to lower-bit representations like 8-bit integers. This allows models to run faster and use less memory, making them suitable for resource-constrained devices.

We will also explore the **PyTorch Quantization API**, which provides tools for applying quantization techniques to neural networks in an easy and structured way. This section will show how to take advantage of the API to quantize models and improve their performance without sacrificing much accuracy.

Lastly, we will revisit **mixed precision training** and the use of **AMP** to further optimize inference times. By combining quantization and AMP, we will learn how to strike the right balance between speed, memory efficiency, and model performance, which is critical for deploying models at scale.

Introduction to Model Quantization

Model quantization is a crucial technique in deep learning that enables efficient deployment of neural networks, especially when running models on resource-constrained devices like mobile phones, IoT devices, and edge computing environments. As deep learning models have grown in complexity and size, running them efficiently on limited hardware has become a challenge. Quantization offers a solution by reducing the numerical precision of the weights and activations in a model, resulting in smaller model sizes and faster inference times, all while maintaining acceptable levels of accuracy. This process is key in enabling real-time AI applications on devices with limited computational resources.

At its core, quantization converts 32-bit floating-point numbers, which are typically used for training neural networks, into lower-precision formats like 16-bit, 8-bit, or even integer formats such as **int8** or **int4**. By reducing the precision of the computations, the model consumes less memory and can be processed faster by hardware accelerators optimized for lower-precision arithmetic, such as modern CPUs, GPUs, and specialized AI chips like **NVIDIA Tensor Cores** and **Google's TPUs**.

Quantization has gained widespread adoption in the AI community due to its practical benefits. Many experts see it as a critical tool for enabling AI on edge devices and resource-constrained environments. According to **William Dally**, Chief Scientist at NVIDIA, "Quantization is key to bringing AI from the data center to mobile and edge devices. As hardware continues to evolve, more advanced quantization techniques will make it possible to run even the most complex AI models efficiently on devices we use every day."

Similarly, **Geoffrey Hinton**, one of the pioneers of deep learning, noted the importance of quantization in future AI applications. "Efficient deployment of neural networks is the next big challenge in AI, and quantization is at the heart of solving that problem. We need models that are not only accurate but also capable of running on the devices people have in their hands."

Why Quantization for Deployment?

As deep learning models continue to grow in size and complexity, deploying these models on devices with limited computational resources has become a significant challenge. Quantization addresses several of the key issues faced during deployment:

- **Reduced Model Size**: Quantized models require less memory, making it easier to deploy models on edge devices like smartphones, smart cameras, and IoT devices. For example, converting weights from 32-bit floats to 8-bit integers can reduce the model size by 4x, which is crucial for devices with limited storage.
- **Improved Inference Speed**: Lower precision arithmetic (such as 8-bit integer operations) is significantly faster than 32-bit floating-point operations on most hardware. This speedup is particularly important for real-time applications like voice assistants, facial recognition, and autonomous driving, where low latency is crucial.
- **Lower Power Consumption**: Quantization also helps reduce the power consumption of models, which is essential for battery-operated devices. Performing lower-precision computations requires less energy, allowing models to run more efficiently on mobile devices and embedded systems.

Recent Innovations and Trends in Quantization

The deep learning community has been actively researching new quantization methods to push the boundaries of efficiency without sacrificing accuracy. Some of the recent innovations include:

- **Int4 Quantization**: New hardware, such as **NVIDIA's A100 GPUs**, now supports **int4** (4-bit integer) operations, offering even greater reductions in model size and computation time compared to traditional int8 quantization. While this represents a significant advancement in performance, it requires highly specialized techniques to ensure that the accuracy loss remains minimal when using such low precision.
- **Adaptive Quantization**: Recent research has focused on **adaptive quantization**, which dynamically adjusts the precision of different layers based on their importance. For instance, layers that are critical to maintaining model accuracy remain in higher precision, while less important layers are quantized more aggressively. This approach allows for a better trade-off between efficiency and performance.
- **Learned Quantization**: Another recent development is **learned quantization**, where the quantization parameters (e.g., scaling factors) are learned during training, rather than being fixed. This method enables more fine-grained control over how the model handles low precision, improving robustness to quantization.
- **Hardware-Aware Quantization**: There has been increasing focus on **hardware-aware**

quantization, where the quantization strategy is designed specifically to take advantage of the capabilities of the deployment hardware. For instance, some accelerators are optimized for 8-bit operations, while others might excel at handling mixed precision. Tailoring the quantization approach to the hardware allows for maximum efficiency during inference.

- **Quantization for Transformers and BERT**: There has been significant interest in quantizing transformer models like **BERT** and **GPT-3**. These models are large and computationally expensive, making them ideal candidates for quantization. Recent research has shown that quantizing transformer layers can dramatically reduce inference times without significantly affecting the model's performance in NLP tasks.

How Quantization Works?

Quantization involves mapping the high-precision values of model parameters (such as weights and biases) and activations to lower-precision representations. During this process, some granularity is lost, but careful techniques ensure that the impact on model performance is minimal. Quantization can be applied to various parts of the model, including:

- **Weights**: Converting the trained 32-bit weights into lower-precision formats.
- **Activations**: Reducing the precision of activations during inference to speed up the computation.
- **Gradients**: Although less common, quantization can be applied during the backward pass (training) to improve training efficiency.

Quantization is typically applied after a model has been trained. This is called **`post-training quantization (PTQ)`**, which allows for optimizations without altering the training process itself. However, **`quantization-aware training (QAT)`** is another technique that incorporates quantization during the training process, resulting in a model that is more robust to the lower-precision format and performs better when quantized.

Techniques for Model Quantization

There are several techniques used for model quantization, each offering different trade-offs between speed, accuracy, and memory efficiency. The most common methods include:

- **PTQ**: This technique quantizes a pre-trained model after it has been fully trained. It is easy to apply and is suitable for a wide range of use cases, especially when the accuracy loss is acceptable. The model weights and activations are quantized from 32-bit to 8-bit integers. PTQ is widely used because it doesn't require retraining the model and can lead to substantial reductions in model size and inference time.
- **QAT**: In QAT, the model is trained with quantization in mind. This means that the forward pass is performed using fake quantization during training, simulating the effects of quantization on weights and activations while maintaining the high precision necessary for backpropagation. QAT tends to produce models that are more robust to quantization,

often with minimal accuracy loss. It's particularly useful when post-training quantization leads to significant performance degradation.

- **Dynamic Quantization**: Dynamic quantization only applies quantization to certain parts of the model, particularly during inference. For example, the model's weights might remain in high precision during training, but during inference, activations are quantized dynamically to reduce memory usage and speed up computation. Dynamic quantization is especially useful for models like transformers in NLP tasks, where parts of the model, such as the weights of fully connected layers, can be quantized without much accuracy loss.
- **Integer-Only Quantization**: This technique converts both weights and activations to integer values, avoiding floating-point calculations altogether. It is particularly suited for hardware that doesn't have dedicated floating-point processing units. Integer-only quantization is frequently used in mobile and embedded devices, where both memory and compute resources are limited.
- **Mixed Precision Quantization**: Some modern quantization techniques combine both high- and low-precision arithmetic to achieve a balance between speed and accuracy. For example, critical layers in the model might remain in 32-bit or 16-bit precision, while less sensitive layers are quantized to 8-bit or even 4-bit. Mixed precision quantization can offer the best of both worlds by improving efficiency while minimizing the loss of accuracy.

Recent experiments in industry and academia have demonstrated the effectiveness of quantization across various domains. **`Google's TensorFlow Lite`** and **`NVIDIA TensorRT`** are two prominent frameworks that offer quantization for real-time AI applications. Their success in reducing model size and improving speed has made quantization a widely adopted practice in deploying machine learning models for production.

Using PyTorch Quantization API

`The PyTorch Quantization API` provides a straightforward and powerful set of tools for performing model quantization. It allows for both PTQ and QAT. With this API, developers can easily convert their models to lower precision, enabling more efficient inference, especially on edge devices and resource-constrained hardware. Quantization in PyTorch supports int8 precision and allows models to be optimized without significant accuracy loss.

Introduction to PyTorch Quantization API

PyTorch's quantization workflow provides flexibility for different quantization strategies, including:

- **Dynamic Quantization**: Applies quantization during inference, dynamically converting weights and activations to lower precision.
- **Post-Training Static Quantization (PTQ)**: Quantizes the model after it has been fully trained, using calibration data to fine-tune the quantization process.

- **QAT**: Simulates quantization during training, making the model more robust when quantized.

In this section, we will focus on **QAT**, which typically yields the highest accuracy for quantized models. QAT allows the model to be trained while taking quantization into account, ensuring that the quantized model performs well on lower-precision hardware.

QAT with PyTorch

Now that our environment is ready, we will apply QAT to the neural network model developed in previous chapters. QAT allows us to simulate the effects of quantization during training, enabling the model to adapt and remain accurate after quantization.

Prepare Model for Quantization

The first step in quantizing a model with PyTorch is to define the quantization configuration. We will configure the model to use **fake quantization** during training, which mimics the behavior of quantized weights and activations.

```
import torch

import torch.nn as nn

import torch.quantization as quantization


# Define the custom model (from previous sections) for
quantization-aware training

class QuantizableFishNet(nn.Module):

   def __init__(self, input_size, hidden_size,
output_size):

       super(QuantizableFishNet, self).__init__()

       self.custom_layer = nn.Linear(input_size,
hidden_size)

       self.fc1 = nn.Linear(hidden_size, hidden_size)

       self.fc2 = nn.Linear(hidden_size, output_size)
```

```
        self.relu = nn.ReLU()

        # Add quantization stubs
        self.quant = quantization.QuantStub()  #
Placeholder for quantized input
        self.dequant = quantization.DeQuantStub()  #
Placeholder for dequantized output

    def forward(self, x):
        # Quantize the input
        x = self.quant(x)
        x = self.custom_layer(x)
        x = self.relu(self.fc1(x))
        x = self.fc2(x)
        # Dequantize the output
        x = self.dequant(x)
        return x

# Initialize the quantizable model
model = QuantizableFishNet(input_size=5, hidden_size=10,
output_size=1)
```

In the above script, we added **QuantStub** and **DeQuantStub**, which are used to quantize the input and dequantize the output during training. These stubs allow us to simulate quantization in the forward pass, ensuring that the model adapts to lower-precision operations.

Fuse Model Layers for Quantization

Layer fusion is a technique that combines adjacent layers (e.g., convolution followed by ReLU) to reduce the overhead and improve performance during quantization. PyTorch's quantization API provides a simple way to fuse layers before training.

```
# Fuse layers that can be combined during quantization

model_fused = torch.quantization.fuse_modules(model,
[['custom_layer', 'fc1', 'relu']])
```

In this case, we are fusing the custom layer, fully connected layer, and ReLU activation to improve performance after quantization.

Configure Quantization Settings

Now, we will configure the quantization process by specifying the type of quantization we want to perform and preparing the model for QAT.

```
# Set the model to use QAT with a specific configuration

model.qconfig =
torch.quantization.get_default_qat_qconfig('fbgemm')



# Prepare the model for quantization-aware training

model_prepared =
torch.quantization.prepare_qat(model_fused)
```

The **`QConfig`** (quantization configuration) determines how weights and activations will be quantized. In this example, we are using the default **`fbgemm`** backend, which is optimized for x86 platforms and is widely used for QAT.

Training Model with QAT

With the model now prepared for QAT, we can train it as usual, while PyTorch simulates quantized operations during the forward pass. This allows the model to adjust to the lower precision, minimizing accuracy loss when fully quantized.

```
# Define the loss function and optimizer
criterion = nn.MSELoss()
optimizer = torch.optim.Adam(model_prepared.parameters(),
lr=0.001)

# Dummy training loop
num_epochs = 50
for epoch in range(num_epochs):
   model_prepared.train()
   optimizer.zero_grad()

   # Forward pass
   outputs = model_prepared(X_train_tensor)
   loss = criterion(outputs, y_train_tensor.unsqueeze(1))

   # Backward pass and optimization
   loss.backward()
   optimizer.step()

   if (epoch + 1) % 10 == 0:
       print(f'Epoch [{epoch+1}/{num_epochs}], Loss:
{loss.item():.4f}')
```

During training, the quantized version of the model (using fake quantization) is trained in a way that it can later be converted to an actual quantized model for deployment.

Convert Model to Quantized Version

After training, we can convert the model to a fully quantized version using **convert()**.

```
# Convert the model to a fully quantized version

model_quantized =
torch.quantization.convert(model_prepared)
```

This step converts the weights and activations from floating-point to 8-bit integer format, resulting in a model that is smaller and faster during inference.

Evaluate Quantized Model

Now that the model has been quantized, we can evaluate its performance on the test dataset to ensure that it performs well in its quantized form.

```
# Evaluate the quantized model

model_quantized.eval()

with torch.no_grad():

   test_outputs = model_quantized(X_test_tensor)

   test_loss = criterion(test_outputs,
y_test_tensor.unsqueeze(1))

   print(f'Test Loss: {test_loss.item():.4f}')
```

By quantizing the model, we significantly reduce its size and speed up inference, making it suitable for deployment on edge devices or systems with limited computational resources.

Mixed Precision Training and AMP

Mixed Precision Training and AMP offer a powerful approach to optimizing both training and inference by using a combination of 16-bit and 32-bit floating-point precision. While mixed precision is often discussed in the context of speeding up training, its benefits extend to inference as well, making it a valuable tool for improving the efficiency of deep learning models during deployment. With AMP, you can perform calculations in lower precision without significant accuracy loss, allowing models to run faster and with reduced memory consumption.

How AMP Accelerates Inference

AMP leverages the ability of modern hardware, such as **NVIDIA GPUs with Tensor Cores**, to handle **half-precision (float16)** computations efficiently. By performing a significant portion of the calculations in lower precision (float16) while keeping critical parts of the model, like loss functions and gradient calculations, in full precision (float32), AMP accelerates the overall computation without sacrificing the accuracy of the final results.

During inference, the model no longer performs backpropagation or gradient calculations, but it still processes a large number of matrix operations (such as those in fully connected layers, convolutional layers, and attention mechanisms). By applying AMP, these operations can be executed faster, especially in models with heavy computation demands, such as **transformers**, **CNNs**, and the custom neural network model we've developed.

Benefits of AMP in Inference

- **Speed Improvements**: Performing inference in **mixed precision** enables faster calculations, as 16-bit precision (float16) operations are more efficient on modern GPUs, especially those with Tensor Cores, compared to 32-bit floating-point operations. The speedup can be particularly noticeable in large models, where most of the computation can be handled in lower precision.
- **Memory Efficiency**: Using lower precision for many operations during inference reduces the memory footprint. This allows models to fit more easily into the memory of resource-constrained devices or to handle larger batch sizes on the same hardware. In environments where memory is limited, such as mobile devices or embedded systems, AMP enables efficient deployment.
- **No Accuracy Trade-offs**: One of the most significant advantages of AMP is its ability to maintain model accuracy. Through careful management of precision, PyTorch ensures that critical computations, such as the final layers and certain matrix operations, remain in 32-bit precision, where necessary, to prevent any accuracy degradation. As a result, inference speed is improved without sacrificing performance or reliability.

AMP for Neural Network Model

For the **FishNet** model and other advanced architectures, we've developed, AMP can significantly enhance the inference process. When deploying this model to production, particularly on hardware with Tensor Cores, the model can take advantage of mixed precision to reduce inference time, which is crucial for real-time applications like image recognition or real-time recommendation systems.

Given below is how AMP improves inference in our neural network model:

- **Convolutional layers** (if used in extended architectures) and **fully connected layers** perform a large number of matrix multiplications and can benefit from reduced precision without impacting accuracy. By applying AMP, these operations are executed in float16 precision, speeding up computation.
- **Transformer-based architectures** rely heavily on matrix multiplications, particularly in **multi-head attention** mechanisms. AMP allows these complex calculations to run more efficiently, which is essential for sequence-based tasks like natural language processing and time-series forecasting.
- For models that use **custom layers**, like our neural network, AMP ensures that lower precision is used wherever possible, while critical parts of the model that affect accuracy, such as output layers and loss calculations, remain in higher precision (float32).

The use of AMP for inference has seen widespread adoption in various industries, particularly in applications requiring real-time AI deployment. Leading companies in the AI space, such as **NVIDIA** and **Google**, have incorporated mixed precision into their production workflows to enhance the scalability and efficiency of deep learning models.

For example:

- **NVIDIA's TensorRT** framework uses AMP to optimize inference on deep learning models deployed on GPUs. By lowering precision where possible, TensorRT has achieved substantial performance gains in applications like self-driving cars, video processing, and speech recognition.
- **Google's Cloud AI** services have integrated AMP to allow developers to deploy models that are not only faster but also more cost-effective, as they require less compute power for the same level of performance.

AMP Use-cases for Inference

AMP is particularly valuable in scenarios where **real-time inference** is required, or where hardware resources are limited, such as:

- **Edge and Mobile Devices**: Running models on edge devices like smartphones, IoT devices, or smart cameras often requires a balance between performance and resource usage. AMP makes it possible to deploy complex models on such devices without compromising speed or memory efficiency.
- **Cloud-based Applications**: In cloud environments, where large-scale inference is performed (e.g., in recommendation engines, speech recognition, or translation services), reducing inference time per query can lead to significant cost savings. By reducing the precision for certain operations, AMP allows cloud-based models to process more queries per second on the same hardware.
- **Autonomous Systems**: For systems like self-driving cars or drones, where low latency and real-time decision-making are essential, AMP offers a way to meet stringent

performance requirements while maintaining the model's accuracy and reliability.

While AMP provides significant benefits in terms of speed and memory efficiency, there are a few considerations to keep in mind:

- **Hardware Support**: AMP relies on hardware that supports mixed precision, such as NVIDIA GPUs with Tensor Cores. On CPUs or older GPUs without mixed precision support, the benefits of AMP may not be as pronounced, or the feature might not be available at all.
- **Model Structure**: While most modern models and architectures benefit from AMP, certain layers or operations might not be well-suited for mixed precision. In such cases, PyTorch handles these layers in full precision to avoid accuracy loss, but this can lead to a smaller overall speedup than expected.

Summary

In this chapter, the focus was on quantization and optimization techniques that improve the efficiency of neural networks, especially for deployment on resource-constrained devices. The concept of model quantization was introduced, where the precision of weights and activations is reduced, typically from 32-bit floating-point to lower bit formats like 8-bit integers. This process significantly reduces model size and increases inference speed without substantial accuracy loss. Various quantization techniques were explored, such as PTQ and QAT, both of which offer different strategies for optimizing models.

The PyTorch Quantization API was then introduced, showing how it can be used to perform quantization-aware training. This involved setting up and configuring the environment, preparing the model for quantization, and training it to ensure robustness at lower precision. Using the API, we were able to simulate the effects of quantization during training, allowing the model to adjust and maintain accuracy when converted to its final quantized form.

Finally, the chapter turned to **AMP** and how it accelerates both training and inference by leveraging lower precision operations. AMP enables models to use a combination of 16-bit and 32-bit precision, improving speed and memory efficiency, particularly on GPUs with Tensor Cores. These optimizations are critical for deploying AI models in production environments where resource efficiency is paramount, such as on mobile devices or in real-time applications.

Chapter 7: Migrating TensorFlow to PyTorch

Overview

In this chapter, we will explore the process of migrating models and training pipelines from **TensorFlow** to **PyTorch**, a transition many developers and researchers undertake as PyTorch continues to grow in popularity. We will begin by highlighting the **key differences** between TensorFlow and PyTorch, particularly in terms of their computational models, development workflows, and deployment strategies. Understanding these differences will set the foundation for effectively migrating models and optimizing workflows.

Next, we will dive into **ONNX**, an open-source format that allows models to be easily transferred between frameworks. By understanding how ONNX operates, we can streamline the migration of TensorFlow models to PyTorch, preserving both the model architecture and trained weights.

We will then work through a **practical demonstration** using ONNX to migrate a TensorFlow model to PyTorch, ensuring the model's integrity during the transition. Lastly, we will cover the steps required to migrate **training pipelines and optimizers** from TensorFlow to PyTorch, focusing on how to replicate training strategies, optimization algorithms, and other processes essential for maintaining model performance in the new framework. This chapter aims to provide a smooth pathway for those looking to transition their deep learning projects from TensorFlow to PyTorch.

TensorFlow vs PyTorch Models

Background

Over the past several years, **TensorFlow** and **PyTorch** have emerged as two of the most dominant frameworks for building neural networks and conducting deep learning research. Both have been widely used across academia and industry, driving the development of cutting-edge AI models and systems. However, the landscape has shifted, with **PyTorch** gaining substantial momentum and becoming the preferred framework for many developers and researchers, while TensorFlow's usage has seen a relative decline in certain communities.

TensorFlow, developed by **Google Brain**, was released in 2015 and quickly gained widespread adoption due to its scalability and deployment capabilities, especially for production-level applications. TensorFlow introduced a robust ecosystem of tools and libraries, making it suitable for a variety of tasks ranging from research to deployment across platforms like **TensorFlow Lite**, **TensorFlow Serving**, and **TensorFlow.js**. Its ability to handle large-scale deep learning models and its compatibility with production environments made it a popular choice for enterprises. However, as the framework grew, users often found it difficult to work with due to its steep learning curve and complex debugging process, especially in earlier versions. The use of **static computational graphs** made it harder for developers to experiment with model architectures dynamically, a requirement for many research-focused projects.

In contrast, **PyTorch**, developed by **Facebook's AI Research (FAIR)**, was released in 2016 and has seen rapid growth, particularly in academic and research communities. One of PyTorch's key advantages is its ease of use and **dynamic computational graph** system, which offers more flexibility for developers, making it simpler to experiment with and iterate over complex neural network architectures. As a result, PyTorch has become the framework of choice for deep learning researchers who prioritize flexibility, clear syntax, and an intuitive debugging process.

Growth of PyTorch and Decline of TensorFlow

The shift toward PyTorch began in the academic community, where researchers preferred its dynamic nature, which aligns closely with Python's imperative programming model. PyTorch's popularity surged because it allowed developers to write models in a more Pythonic way, executing code line-by-line and providing immediate feedback. This was in contrast to TensorFlow's static graph approach, which required defining the entire computational graph before running the model.

As a result, many leading research institutions, including **OpenAI**, **DeepMind**, and **Uber AI Labs**, transitioned to PyTorch for developing state-of-the-art models. The adoption of PyTorch in academic settings also influenced its growth in industry, as the models and techniques pioneered in research were easier to port to industry applications. PyTorch's integration with **TorchScript** (which enables models to be exported to production environments) further reduced the gap between research and production, addressing one of the key areas where TensorFlow previously had an advantage.

TensorFlow, despite its continued use in production and large-scale enterprise systems, started facing challenges due to its complexity, especially for new users and researchers. Although TensorFlow 2.x introduced eager execution, which mimicked PyTorch's dynamic graph capabilities, many users had already transitioned to PyTorch by that time. Additionally, PyTorch's stronger community support, better documentation, and integration with modern hardware like **NVIDIA Tensor Cores** further solidified its position as the leading framework for deep learning.

TensorFlow vs. PyTorch

Both frameworks serve the same fundamental purpose: to build, train, and deploy neural networks. However, their approaches to this task differ significantly, particularly in terms of computational graphs, programming paradigms, and overall flexibility. Understanding these differences is critical when considering the migration from TensorFlow to PyTorch.

Static vs. Dynamic

The most notable distinction between TensorFlow and PyTorch lies in how they handle **computational graphs**, which represent the flow of operations in a neural network.

- **TensorFlow's Static Computational Graph**: TensorFlow originally used a **static computational graph** (also known as a define-and-run paradigm). In this approach, the entire computational graph must be defined upfront before it is executed. This graph is a dataflow graph, where nodes represent operations, and edges represent tensors (data) flowing between operations. Once the graph is defined, it can be run multiple times with different input data, but the structure of the graph cannot be altered during execution.
- The advantage of a static graph is that it can be optimized ahead of time. TensorFlow can perform various optimizations like operation fusion, memory optimization, and distributing computation across multiple devices (CPUs, GPUs, or TPUs). Static graphs also make it easier to deploy models to production environments, as the entire graph is serialized and deployed as a single unit.
- However, this approach comes with drawbacks, particularly during model development and experimentation. Modifying the graph requires re-defining and re-compiling it, which can be cumbersome and slow. Debugging is also challenging because errors often occur during graph execution rather than graph definition, making it harder to trace issues in the code.
- **PyTorch's Dynamic Computational Graph**: PyTorch, on the other hand, employs a **dynamic computational graph** (also called a define-by-run paradigm). In this approach, the computational graph is built dynamically as the model executes. This means that each time the model is run, PyTorch constructs the graph on the fly, allowing for greater flexibility and easier debugging.
- The dynamic nature of PyTorch's graph makes it more intuitive and Pythonic. Developers can use standard Python control flow (like loops, conditionals, and function calls) within the graph definition, and they can see the results immediately without needing to pre-define the entire graph. This real-time feedback is invaluable during experimentation, as it allows for quick iteration over different model architectures and debugging.
- While the dynamic graph is not as easily optimized as a static graph, PyTorch's **TorchScript** offers a solution by converting dynamic graphs into static graphs for deployment, bridging the gap between research and production.

Declarative vs. Imperative

Another major difference between TensorFlow and PyTorch is the programming paradigm they adopt.

- **TensorFlow's Declarative Paradigm**: In TensorFlow (especially pre-2.x versions), the model's structure is declared in advance, and the computational graph is built separately from the execution. This means that the developer defines the operations and their dependencies first, then uses a session to execute the graph with specific inputs.
- This declarative approach is useful for optimizing and reusing graphs, but it adds complexity to the code. Developers need to manage sessions and feeds manually, making the learning curve steeper for new users. Moreover, the separation between graph definition and execution can make debugging more difficult, as errors typically surface

during execution rather than during graph construction.

- TensorFlow 2.x has shifted toward eager execution, which allows operations to be executed immediately, similar to PyTorch's imperative model. However, the framework's underlying declarative nature still persists in many areas, particularly when exporting models for deployment.
- **PyTorch's Imperative Paradigm**: PyTorch adopts an **imperative programming model**, which means that operations are executed immediately as they are called. This makes the development process more intuitive and aligns closely with standard Python programming. As a result, PyTorch code is typically easier to write, debug, and understand.
- PyTorch's imperative paradigm simplifies experimentation, as developers can see the results of their code immediately, without needing to predefine the entire graph. The line-by-line execution also makes it easier to integrate PyTorch models with other Python libraries, such as **NumPy** and **SciPy**. Additionally, PyTorch's support for native Python features like conditionals and loops allows for more complex, dynamic models to be built with minimal overhead.

Debugging and Flexibility

When it comes to debugging and flexibility, PyTorch has a clear advantage over TensorFlow, particularly for research and development. The static nature of TensorFlow's computational graph means that debugging can be challenging. Errors often occur during the execution phase rather than during graph definition, making it harder to trace issues back to the source code. TensorFlow's session-based execution model also adds complexity, as developers need to manage variables, sessions, and placeholders, all of which can make it difficult to pinpoint the root cause of an error.

TensorFlow 2.x introduced eager execution to alleviate some of these issues, allowing developers to execute operations immediately and see the results, much like PyTorch. However, debugging in TensorFlow still requires more effort compared to PyTorch, particularly when working with large-scale models.

Whereas, PyTorch's dynamic computational graph makes debugging significantly easier. Because operations are executed immediately, developers can use Python's native debugging tools (like **pdb**) to inspect tensors, variables, and operations as they occur. This real-time feedback allows for quick iteration and experimentation, making PyTorch the preferred choice for researchers and developers who need to test new ideas rapidly.

Moreover, PyTorch's tight integration with Python means that it is easy to incorporate other libraries and tools into the development process, further enhancing its flexibility.

Deployment and Scalability

While PyTorch has historically been favored for research and development, TensorFlow was the go-to framework for deploying models at scale, particularly in production environments.

- **TensorFlow**: TensorFlow's static computational graph and extensive ecosystem make it well-suited for deployment in production environments. TensorFlow's tools, such as **TensorFlow Serving**, **TensorFlow Lite**, and **TensorFlow.js**, provide comprehensive solutions for deploying models across a wide range of platforms, from mobile devices to web browsers. TensorFlow's support for **TPUs** (Tensor Processing Units) also gives it an edge in certain high-performance production scenarios.
- **PyTorch**: While PyTorch was initially seen as a research-oriented framework, the introduction of **TorchScript** has made it easier to deploy models in production environments. TorchScript allows developers to convert dynamic PyTorch models into static graphs, enabling optimizations and compatibility with production systems. PyTorch has also integrated with platforms like **ONNX** to facilitate model export and deployment.

In recent years, PyTorch has narrowed the gap between research and production, making it an increasingly viable option for end-to-end deep learning workflows, from experimentation to deployment.

Exploring ONXX

ONNX is an open-source format designed to facilitate interoperability between different deep learning frameworks. Initially developed by **Microsoft** and **Facebook**, ONNX has gained widespread adoption and is now supported by major AI platforms, including **PyTorch**, **TensorFlow**, **Caffe2**, and others. The primary purpose of ONNX is to allow developers to train models in one framework, such as TensorFlow or PyTorch, and then export them to another framework or deployment environment without the need for significant modifications. This cross-compatibility is invaluable in scenarios where a model might be developed in a research setting using PyTorch but needs to be deployed in a production environment that uses TensorFlow, for example.

Purpose of ONNX

ONNX solves a fundamental problem in deep learning: the inability to move models seamlessly between frameworks. In the past, models trained in one framework were often locked into that ecosystem, making it difficult to transfer them to different production environments or leverage different tools for inference and deployment. ONNX addresses this by providing a standardized format for representing deep learning models. It ensures that once a model is trained, it can be exported to a variety of environments, including cloud services, edge devices, and mobile platforms, all while preserving the model's architecture, weights, and computation graph.

By using ONNX, developers can:

- **Switch Between Frameworks**: Train a model in one framework (e.g., PyTorch) and export it to another (e.g., TensorFlow or Caffe2) for inference or further development.
- **Deploy Models Efficiently**: Once a model is exported in ONNX format, it can be

deployed on a variety of hardware platforms, such as CPUs, GPUs, and specialized hardware like **TPUs** or **NVIDIA TensorRT**.

- **Optimize Models**: Many hardware vendors, such as **NVIDIA**, provide optimizations specifically for ONNX models, allowing faster inference on their platforms without having to modify the model's architecture.

ONNX also simplifies the **`model deployment pipeline`** by supporting a unified format that works across different platforms. Developers no longer need to worry about whether a model developed in one framework can be efficiently deployed on another, as ONNX serves as the bridge.

Key Achievements of ONNX

Since its inception, ONNX has played a significant role in bridging the gap between frameworks and deployment environments. Some of its key achievements include:

- **Widespread Adoption**: ONNX has been adopted by many major players in the deep learning ecosystem, including cloud providers like **Microsoft Azure**, **AWS**, and **Google Cloud**, as well as hardware vendors like **Intel**, **NVIDIA**, and **ARM**. Its support across diverse platforms makes it a reliable format for production use.
- **Interoperability Between Frameworks**: ONNX has allowed models to be shared across popular frameworks like PyTorch and TensorFlow, streamlining workflows for researchers and engineers. The ability to move a model from one framework to another is especially useful in cases where certain frameworks have unique strengths in specific domains (e.g., PyTorch for research and TensorFlow for production).
- **Optimization for Inference**: ONNX allows for model optimization at inference time. Hardware vendors have built specialized inference engines, like **NVIDIA's TensorRT** and **Intel's OpenVINO**, that can process ONNX models more efficiently. These optimizations often result in significant speedups in inference, making ONNX ideal for real-time applications like image recognition, speech processing, and recommendation systems.
- **Growing Ecosystem**: The ONNX ecosystem continues to expand with the introduction of tools like **ONNX Runtime**, an optimized inference engine that accelerates the execution of models on different hardware backends. This framework-agnostic approach ensures that models can be deployed on the most suitable hardware for a given task.

ONNX Format

At its core, ONNX represents deep learning models using a computational graph format. The model is defined as a directed acyclic graph (DAG) where nodes represent operations (e.g., convolution, pooling, matrix multiplication), and edges represent the flow of data between these operations (i.e., tensors). The ONNX format encapsulates both the structure of the model and its associated parameters, such as weights and biases.

ONNX defines a variety of operators that are commonly used in neural network models, including layers for convolutions, batch normalization, activation functions, and fully connected layers. It also supports custom operators, which allow developers to extend the format for operations specific to their use case.

An ONNX model is structured into several key components:

- **Graph**: The graph defines the model architecture. Each node in the graph corresponds to an operation or layer in the neural network, while the edges represent tensors flowing between operations.
- **Nodes**: Each node defines an operation, such as a **convolution**, **ReLU**, or **matmul**. The inputs and outputs for each node are tensors.
- **Inputs and Outputs**: The model defines input and output tensors that represent the data flowing into and out of the computational graph.
- **Parameters**: The model stores parameters such as weights and biases, which are required to execute the graph. These are usually exported from the framework where the model was originally trained.
- **Metadata**: Additional metadata, such as the model version and framework used to create the model, are also included.

We will now illustrate the process of exporting a pretrained neural network model to ONNX format using PyTorch.

Exporting Pretrained NN Model to ONNX

PyTorch provides built-in support for exporting models to ONNX format. The process is straightforward and involves specifying the model and a sample input tensor to trace the computation graph. We will walk through exporting a simple pretrained model, such as **`ResNet18`**, to ONNX format.

Load Pretrained Model in PyTorch

We will begin by loading a pretrained ResNet18 model from PyTorch's model zoo. The model is available in the following URL:

https://github.com/pytorch/vision/blob/main/torchvision/models/resnet.py

```
import torch

import torchvision.models as models



# Load a pretrained ResNet18 model
```

```
model = models.resnet18(pretrained=True)


# Set the model to evaluation mode (since we are
exporting for inference)

model.eval()
```

Create Sample Input Tensor

To export the model, we need to provide a sample input tensor that matches the input size expected by the model. For ResNet18, this would typically be a 3-channel image of size 224x224:

```
# Create a dummy input tensor (batch size of 1, 3 color
channels, 224x224 image)

dummy_input = torch.randn(1, 3, 224, 224)
```

Export Model to ONNX Format

We can now export the model to ONNX using PyTorch's **torch.onnx.export()** function. This function traces the model's computation graph with the provided input and outputs the ONNX representation of the model:

```
# Export the model to ONNX format

torch.onnx.export(

   model,                      # Model to export

   dummy_input,                 # Dummy input to trace the
model

   "resnet18.onnx",             # Output file path

   export_params=True,          # Store trained parameters
(weights and biases)

   opset_version=11,            # ONNX opset version
```

```
    do_constant_folding=True,    # Fold constants for
optimization
    input_names=['input'],       # Input node names
    output_names=['output'],     # Output node names
    dynamic_axes={'input': {0: 'batch_size'}, 'output':
{0: 'batch_size'}}  # Dynamic batch size
)
```

This above function performs the following:

- **Tracing the Model**: The input tensor is used to trace the model's computation graph, capturing all operations and data flows.
- **Exporting Parameters**: The **export_params=True** flag ensures that the model's trained parameters (weights and biases) are included in the ONNX file.
- **Opset Version**: The **opset_version=11** specifies the version of ONNX's operator set to use, ensuring compatibility with modern frameworks.
- **Dynamic Axes**: The **dynamic_axes** option allows for dynamic batch sizes, making the model more flexible when deployed.

Verify ONNX Model

Once the model is exported, we can use the **onnx** package to load and inspect the model:

```
import onnx


# Load the ONNX model
onnx_model = onnx.load("resnet18.onnx")


# Check the model for any inconsistencies
onnx.checker.check_model(onnx_model)
```

```
# Print a human-readable representation of the model

print(onnx.helper.printable_graph(onnx_model.graph))
```

The ONNX format now encapsulates both the architecture and weights of the ResNet18 model. It can be loaded into any compatible framework or runtime for inference. Through this example, we were able to experience how easy it was to leverage ONNX for deep learning projects.

Sample Program: Using ONXX to Migrate TensorFlow Models

For this exercise, we will use a pre-trained **MobileNetV2** model from TensorFlow's model zoo, which is available on GitHub and widely used in mobile and edge applications. MobileNetV2 is a lightweight convolutional neural network that is particularly efficient for classification tasks. We will convert it from TensorFlow to ONNX, and finally load it into PyTorch for inference.

Load TensorFlow MobileNetV2 Model

First, we need to download and load the TensorFlow **MobileNetV2** model. TensorFlow provides pre-trained versions of MobileNetV2 that can be loaded directly through its API. The model is available in the following github url:

https://github.com/tensorflow/models/tree/master/research/slim/nets/mobilenet

```
import tensorflow as tf



# Load the pretrained MobileNetV2 model from TensorFlow

mobilenet_v2 =
tf.keras.applications.MobileNetV2(weights='imagenet')



# Convert the model to a TensorFlow SavedModel format
```

```
mobilenet_v2.save('mobilenet_v2_tf')
```

The **mobilenet_v2** model is pre-trained on the **ImageNet** dataset, and we save it to the **SavedModel** format, which is the default format in TensorFlow for exporting models.

Convert TensorFlow Model to ONNX Format

With the TensorFlow model saved, we can now convert it into the ONNX format using the **tf2onnx** converter. This tool allows us to take a TensorFlow SavedModel and export it to ONNX, making the model compatible with other frameworks like PyTorch.

First, ensure that the **tf2onnx** package is installed:

```
pip install tf2onnx
```

Now, convert the **MobileNetV2** model from TensorFlow to ONNX:

```
python -m tf2onnx.convert --saved-model mobilenet_v2_tf -
-output mobilenet_v2.onnx
```

This command exports the TensorFlow **MobileNetV2** model to ONNX format, which can now be loaded and used in PyTorch or any other framework that supports ONNX.

Checking ONNX Model Conversion

Before using the ONNX model in PyTorch, we should verify that it has been correctly converted. We can do this by loading the ONNX model using the **onnx** package and checking its structure:

```
import onnx


# Load the ONNX model

onnx_model = onnx.load("mobilenet_v2.onnx")


# Check the model for any inconsistencies
```

```
onnx.checker.check_model(onnx_model)


# Print a readable format of the ONNX model's
computational graph

print(onnx.helper.printable_graph(onnx_model.graph))
```

This ensures that the ONNX model has been correctly exported from TensorFlow and is ready for further use.

Load ONNX Model into PyTorch

Now that the TensorFlow model has been converted to ONNX, the next step is to load this ONNX model into PyTorch. We use **onnxruntime** or **torch.onnx** for inference with the ONNX model in PyTorch. For this example, we will use **onnxruntime** to run inference with the ONNX model directly in PyTorch.

To begin with, first load the ONNX model into PyTorch for inference:

```
import onnxruntime

import numpy as np

from PIL import Image

from torchvision import transforms


# Define a function to preprocess the input image

def preprocess_image(image_path):

   input_image = Image.open(image_path).resize((224,
224))

   preprocess = transforms.Compose([

       transforms.Resize(256),
```

```
        transforms.CenterCrop(224),

        transforms.ToTensor(),

        transforms.Normalize(mean=[0.485, 0.456, 0.406],
std=[0.229, 0.224, 0.225]),

    ])

    input_tensor = preprocess(input_image).unsqueeze(0)  #
Create a batch dimension

    return input_tensor.numpy()


# Load the ONNX model using onnxruntime

onnx_session =
onnxruntime.InferenceSession('mobilenet_v2.onnx')


# Get the input and output names for the ONNX model

input_name = onnx_session.get_inputs()[0].name

output_name = onnx_session.get_outputs()[0].name


# Preprocess the input image

input_data = preprocess_image("sample_image.jpg")


# Run the ONNX model using the preprocessed input data

result = onnx_session.run([output_name], {input_name:
input_data})
```

```
# Print the top-5 classification results

print("ONNX Model Inference Results:",
np.argmax(result[0], axis=1))
```

In the above script, we use **onnxruntime** to load the ONNX model and perform inference. The **preprocess_image()** function prepares the input image for the model, resizing and normalizing it as expected by MobileNetV2. And then, we run the ONNX model and print the top-5 predicted classes.

Once the ONNX model is loaded, it can be integrated into any PyTorch pipeline, allowing the pre-trained model to be used for inference or further fine-tuning in PyTorch. PyTorch's flexibility and support for ONNX make it an ideal framework for continuing model development after the migration.

Migrating Training Pipelines and Optimizers

When migrating models from **`TensorFlow`** to **`PyTorch`**, one of the critical aspects is adapting the **`training pipelines`** and **`optimizers`**. The training loop, including loss calculation, backpropagation, and optimization, often differs between TensorFlow and PyTorch due to the frameworks' respective approaches to handling tensors, gradients, and computational graphs. In this section, we will walk through the process of migrating the training pipeline and optimizers for the **`MobileNetV2`** model from TensorFlow to PyTorch, ensuring that the transition is smooth and the model training remains consistent across frameworks.

Migrating TensorFlow Training Pipeline to PyTorch

We will begin by breaking down the training process in both TensorFlow and PyTorch, and then illustrate how to migrate a typical TensorFlow training pipeline to PyTorch using the same **`MobileNetV2`** model example.

In TensorFlow, the training loop for **`MobileNetV2`** could look something like this:

```
import tensorflow as tf



# Load the MobileNetV2 model
```

```
mobilenet_v2 =
tf.keras.applications.MobileNetV2(weights='imagenet')


# Compile the model

mobilenet_v2.compile(optimizer='adam',
loss='categorical_crossentropy', metrics=['accuracy'])


# Example dataset (for simplicity, we are using random
data here)

train_dataset = tf.random.normal([32, 224, 224, 3])  #
Batch of 32 images

train_labels = tf.random.uniform([32], maxval=1000,
dtype=tf.int64)  # Random labels


# Training loop using model.fit() (high-level API)

mobilenet_v2.fit(train_dataset, train_labels, epochs=5)
```

In the above example, **mobilenet_v2.compile()** sets up the optimizer, loss function, and metrics. The **model.fit()** function handles the entire training process, abstracting away the individual steps of forward pass, loss calculation, and optimizer updates.

Also, TensorFlow allows for more granular control using **tf.GradientTape** for custom training loops as shown below:

```
# Manual training loop using GradientTape

optimizer = tf.keras.optimizers.Adam()
```

```
for epoch in range(5):
   with tf.GradientTape() as tape:
        # Forward pass
        logits = mobilenet_v2(train_dataset,
training=True)
        loss_value =
tf.keras.losses.sparse_categorical_crossentropy(train_lab
els, logits)


   # Backpropagation
   grads = tape.gradient(loss_value,
mobilenet_v2.trainable_weights)
   optimizer.apply_gradients(zip(grads,
mobilenet_v2.trainable_weights))


   print(f"Epoch {epoch + 1}: Loss =
{tf.reduce_mean(loss_value)}")
```

In the above manual training loop, **`tf.GradientTape`** captures the gradient information for each training step. And **`tape.gradient()`** computes the gradients, and **`apply_gradients()`** updates the model weights using the optimizer.

Migrating Training Loop to PyTorch

To migrate the training pipeline to PyTorch, we need to adapt the model, loss function, and optimizer. In PyTorch, these components are more explicitly handled in a custom training loop, which gives more control over each step of the process.

Defining PyTorch Model

We will begin by loading the **MobileNetV2** model in PyTorch, either by using a pre-trained version or by converting the TensorFlow model via ONNX (as previously demonstrated):

```
import torch

import torchvision.models as models


# Load pretrained MobileNetV2 model from torchvision

mobilenet_v2 = models.mobilenet_v2(pretrained=True)


# Set the model to training mode

mobilenet_v2.train()
```

Defining Loss Function and Optimizer

We define the loss function and optimizer separately:

```
# Define the loss function and optimizer

criterion = torch.nn.CrossEntropyLoss()

optimizer = torch.optim.Adam(mobilenet_v2.parameters(),
lr=0.001)
```

Writing PyTorch Training Loop

Now, we adapt the TensorFlow training pipeline to PyTorch's explicit training loop:

```
# Example dataset (using random data for demonstration)

train_dataset = torch.randn(32, 3, 224, 224)  # Batch of
32 images

train_labels = torch.randint(0, 1000, (32,))  # Random
labels
```

```
# Training loop
num_epochs = 5
for epoch in range(num_epochs):
   optimizer.zero_grad()  # Clear previous gradients

   # Forward pass
   outputs = mobilenet_v2(train_dataset)
   loss = criterion(outputs, train_labels)  # Compute the
loss

   # Backward pass (calculate gradients)
   loss.backward()

   # Optimization step (update model weights)
   optimizer.step()

   print(f"Epoch {epoch + 1}, Loss: {loss.item():.4f}")
```

In the above PyTorch training loop,

- **`optimizer.zero_grad()`** clears the gradients from the previous iteration.
- The forward pass is executed with **`mobilenet_v2(train_dataset)`**, and the loss is computed using the criterion.
- **`loss.backward()`** calculates the gradients, and **`optimizer.step()`** updates the model parameters.

Migrating Optimizers

TensorFlow and PyTorch both offer a variety of optimization algorithms, including **Adam**, **SGD**, and **RMSProp**. However, the syntax and handling of optimizers differ slightly between the two frameworks.

Optimizers in TensorFlow

In TensorFlow, the optimizer is typically defined as part of the model compilation process, as shown earlier:

```
optimizer = tf.keras.optimizers.Adam(learning_rate=0.001)
```

This optimizer is then used in the training loop, either via **model.fit()** or **apply_gradients()**.

Optimizers in PyTorch

In PyTorch, the optimizer is defined using the **torch.optim** module and explicitly linked to the model's parameters:

```
optimizer = torch.optim.Adam(mobilenet_v2.parameters(),
lr=0.001)
```

The optimizer must be explicitly called in the training loop using **optimizer.step()**, unlike TensorFlow's abstracted handling of backpropagation and updates.

Key Differences in Training Pipelines and Optimizers

Feature	TensorFlow	PyTorch
Model Definition	Defined with tf.keras.Model() or Sequential()	Defined with torch.nn.Module()
Training Loop	Abstracted with **model.fit()** or custom using **GradientTape**	Custom loop using forward, backward, and optimization steps

Optimizer Definition	Abstracted in model.compile() or custom with apply_gradients()	Defined using **torch.optim** and updated manually
Loss Function	Handled during compilation or custom in loop	Defined with **torch.nn** and calculated in loop
Backpropagation	Automatic in high-level API, manual with **GradientTape**	Manual using loss.backward()

You must adapt several key components when migrating a TensorFlow training pipeline to PyTorch: the model definition, the training loop, the loss function, and the optimizer. While TensorFlow abstracts many of these processes in high-level APIs like **model.fit()**, PyTorch gives developers more granular control over each step, which is often preferred in research and development.

Summary

In this chapter, the focus was on the process of migrating TensorFlow models and training pipelines to PyTorch, utilizing the ONNX format to facilitate the transition. The key differences between TensorFlow and PyTorch were highlighted, particularly their approaches to handling computational graphs and programming paradigms. TensorFlow's static computational graph and declarative programming were contrasted with PyTorch's dynamic graph and imperative programming style, which offer more flexibility and control during model development.

The role of ONNX in making this migration process smoother was explored, showcasing its ability to bridge the gap between different frameworks by offering a unified format for models. By converting TensorFlow models, such as MobileNetV2, into ONNX format, we demonstrated how these models can be efficiently transferred to PyTorch for further development and deployment. ONNX's growing ecosystem and its ability to optimize models for inference on various platforms were also explored.

Additionally, the chapter detailed how to adapt TensorFlow's training pipelines and optimizers to PyTorch, showing how the explicit nature of PyTorch's training loop and optimizer updates contrasts with TensorFlow's more abstracted approach. Through practical examples, the steps involved in converting training pipelines and maintaining model performance during migration were demonstrated. This process emphasized the flexibility PyTorch offers while maintaining seamless integration when moving models from TensorFlow.

CHAPTER 8: DEPLOYING PYTORCH MODELS WITH TORCHSERVE

Overview

In this chapter, the focus will be on deploying PyTorch models using **TorchServe**, a tool designed to make the deployment process efficient and scalable. Deploying machine learning models for real-world applications requires moving from the development environment to a production environment, where models need to handle requests, provide predictions, and integrate with larger systems. TorchServe simplifies this process, enabling developers to serve PyTorch models as RESTful APIs for real-time inference.

We will begin by exploring the fundamentals of **model deployment**, understanding the challenges and considerations involved, such as scalability, performance, and integration. Then, we will move on to **setting up TorchServe**, where we will learn how to configure the environment, prepare models for deployment, and run inference using TorchServe's tools. Finally, we will delve into **deploying models for production**, where you will learn how to manage and scale model instances, handle multiple models, and monitor performance for high-traffic production systems. This chapter will provide a comprehensive overview of deploying PyTorch models in a professional production setting using TorchServe.

Exploring Model Deployment

Deploying machine learning models into production environments comes with its own set of challenges. Whether it's a model built for image classification, natural language processing, or recommendation systems, moving from the development environment to production introduces complexities that extend beyond the training process. These challenges stem from the need to ensure that models are both scalable and efficient, while maintaining accuracy, reliability, and security.

Challenges in Model Deployment

One of the most significant challenges in deploying machine learning models is **scalability**. When models are deployed in production, they often need to handle large volumes of requests from users or automated systems. Models that work perfectly well in a controlled development environment can struggle under production loads, where they must provide real-time predictions for potentially thousands or millions of requests. For example, a PyTorch-based model developed for image recognition may need to classify images in real-time in an e-commerce setting, where response time and accuracy directly impact user experience.

Another challenge is **latency and performance optimization**. Machine learning models, particularly deep learning models, can be computationally expensive. They require significant memory and processing power, especially for large datasets or high-dimensional data. In production environments, minimizing inference time is crucial to ensuring smooth performance. For instance, a PyTorch model designed for fraud detection in online transactions must provide near-instant predictions, as delays could lead to poor user experiences or financial losses. Deploying models to environments that support hardware acceleration, such as GPUs or TPUs, can help alleviate these issues, but doing so effectively requires proper integration and optimization.

`Model versioning and updates` are another common pain point. Machine learning models are rarely static—new data, updated algorithms, or refined architectures may require frequent updates to ensure optimal performance. Managing these updates in production without downtime or service disruption can be challenging. For PyTorch models, this could mean retraining on new datasets or tuning hyperparameters and then pushing these updates seamlessly into production.

`Security and reliability` are also paramount in deployment. Machine learning models often process sensitive data, particularly in sectors like healthcare, finance, and autonomous systems. Ensuring that deployed models are secure, don't leak data, and can handle unexpected inputs without failure is crucial. For instance, a PyTorch-based model deployed in a self-driving car needs to remain resilient under all conditions, processing inputs reliably even in challenging environments.

Model Deployment Common Practices

To overcome these challenges, machine learning professionals often rely on expert practices designed to ensure smooth deployment and management of models in production.

- **Containerization and Microservices**: One of the best practices for deploying models is containerization using tools like **Docker** and orchestration platforms like **Kubernetes**. By packaging PyTorch models into containers, developers can ensure that the environment remains consistent from development to production. This reduces the chances of configuration mismatches and makes it easier to scale. Deploying PyTorch models as microservices allows each model to run independently, making it easier to manage updates, scaling, and monitoring.
- **Batching and Caching for Performance Optimization**: To handle high request volumes, developers often implement **batching** techniques, which group multiple inference requests into a single batch for processing. This is especially useful when deploying PyTorch models that rely on GPUs, as it allows better utilization of hardware resources. Additionally, **caching** the results of frequently requested predictions can significantly reduce computation time and improve response times.
- **A/B Testing and Shadow Deployment**: When updating models in production, techniques like **A/B testing** and **shadow deployment** are often employed. A/B testing involves deploying two versions of a model simultaneously and comparing their performance in real-time. Shadow deployment runs the new version of a model alongside the current one without affecting user-facing operations. This practice is useful when deploying updated PyTorch models in production to ensure the newer version performs as expected before it fully replaces the older one.

- **Model Monitoring and Logging**: Continuous monitoring is critical to detect performance degradation, anomalies, or data drift once a model is in production. Tools such as **Prometheus**, **Grafana**, or **TorchServe's native monitoring capabilities** allow ML engineers to track model performance metrics, such as latency, throughput, and prediction accuracy. Logging tools help track failures, unusual patterns, and system utilization, ensuring any issues can be identified and addressed promptly.
- **Hardware Acceleration for Low Latency**: When low latency is a priority, deploying models on hardware accelerators like **NVIDIA GPUs** with **CUDA** support is common. PyTorch models, which are often trained on GPUs, can also benefit from GPU-based inference. For example, a PyTorch-based recommendation system used in an online shopping platform could utilize GPUs in production to generate recommendations quickly based on user data, improving the user experience and supporting higher request volumes.

Several use cases showcase how PyTorch models can be deployed effectively using these best practices. For instance, **Netflix** uses PyTorch models for its recommendation system, utilizing GPUs for real-time inference and containerization for scalability. Similarly, **Tesla's Autopilot** system relies on PyTorch for deploying deep learning models in self-driving cars, ensuring low latency and high reliability by leveraging batching and hardware acceleration.

Another example comes from the **healthcare sector**, where PyTorch models are deployed to process medical images, such as MRI scans, for diagnostic purposes. In this case, containerization and model versioning play critical roles in ensuring that updated models can be rolled out quickly while maintaining patient privacy and data security.

Deploying machine learning models, especially PyTorch ones, requires solving issues related to scalability, performance, and security while ensuring seamless operations in production environments. Adopting expert practices like containerization, model monitoring, and hardware acceleration is essential for ML professionals who want to ensure their models perform efficiently in real-world applications. Together, these practices and tools like TorchServe provide a straightforward approach to deploying and managing PyTorch models in production.

Setting up TorchServe for Inference

TorchServe is a powerful, open-source tool developed by **AWS and Facebook** that allows machine learning practitioners to deploy trained PyTorch models in a scalable, production-ready manner. It provides a standardized way to serve models via a RESTful API, enabling real-time inference, batch processing, and model management. TorchServe simplifies many aspects of deploying models into production, such as model versioning, logging, monitoring, and handling multiple models simultaneously. It's particularly useful for deploying our trained neural network on the **fish dataset**.

TorchServe handles the complexities of model deployment by creating a service that runs in the background, exposing endpoints that receive requests, perform inference on the deployed model, and return predictions in real-time. One of the most significant advantages of using TorchServe is its support for **GPU acceleration**, ensuring low-latency responses for computationally expensive models.

We will now set up TorchServe to deploy the neural network model trained on our fish dataset. This will involve installing TorchServe, packaging the model, and configuring the server for inference.

Installing TorchServe

TorchServe can be installed directly using **pip**. If you haven't installed it already, run the following command to install TorchServe and its model archiver, which is necessary for packaging PyTorch models:

```
pip install torchserve torch-model-archiver
```

Once installed, verify that TorchServe has been correctly installed by checking its version:

```
torchserve --version
```

You should see the installed version of TorchServe displayed, indicating that the installation was successful.

Prepare Trained Model for Deployment

Before deploying the model with TorchServe, we need to package it using the **torch-model-archiver** tool. This tool creates a model archive (.mar file) that TorchServe can load and serve for inference. Our neural network trained on the fish dataset is ready, so we will package it.

Since we have already trained the model as **fishnet.pth**, we now need to create two essential files:

- **model.py**: This file should define the model architecture that matches the one used during training.
- **handler.py**: This file can define custom preprocessing, inference, and post-processing logic (although for standard use, TorchServe provides a default handler).

Creating model.py file

In this file, we will define the same model architecture used during training. Assuming the model architecture is simple, your **model.py** might look like this:

```
import torch.nn as nn

import torch


class FishNet(nn.Module):

   def __init__(self):

       super(FishNet, self).__init__()

       self.layer1 = nn.Linear(5, 10)  # Assuming input
size of 5

       self.layer2 = nn.Linear(10, 1)  # Assuming output
size of 1


   def forward(self, x):

       x = torch.relu(self.layer1(x))

       x = self.layer2(x)

       return x
```

Save this file as **`model.py`** in the same directory where your model weights (**`fishnet.pth`**) are stored.

Packaging Model

Now, use the **`torch-model-archiver`** to create a **`.mar`** file that contains the model's weights, architecture, and other necessary metadata.

```
torch-model-archiver --model-name fishnet --version 1.0 \

   --model-file model.py --serialized-file fishnet.pth \

   --handler torchserve/handlers/image_classifier \
```

```
    --export-path ./model-store --extra-files
index_to_name.json
```

Here,

- **--model-name** specifies the name of the model.
- **--version** indicates the version of the model.
- **--model-file** points to the file defining the model architecture.
- **--serialized-file** points to the **.pth** file that contains the model's trained weights.
- **--handler** specifies the handler for inference. Here, we are using the default image classifier handler.
- **--export-path** specifies the directory where the model archive will be saved.

This command creates a **fishnet.mar** file in the **model-store** directory.

Starting TorchServe

Once the model archive is ready, you can start TorchServe to load and serve the model for inference.

```
torchserve --start --model-store model-store --models
fishnet=fishnet.mar
```

This command starts TorchServe, loads the **fishnet.mar** model from the **model-store**, and makes it available for inference under the name **fishnet**. TorchServe will now listen for incoming inference requests.

Testing Deployed Model

Now that TorchServe is running, we can test the model by sending an inference request to the REST API that TorchServe exposes. For this, create a sample input for the fish dataset model. If the model expects a 5-dimensional input (as indicated in the **model.py** file), you can prepare the input like this:

```
import requests

import json
```

```
# Sample input (replace with actual fish dataset sample)

input_data = [[0.4, 0.7, 1.2, 0.9, 0.5]]


# Prepare the request payload

payload = json.dumps({"data": input_data})


# Send the request to TorchServe's REST API

response =
requests.post("http://127.0.0.1:8080/predictions/fishnet"
, data=payload)


# Print the response

print(response.json())
```

In the above code, **input_data** is a sample input formatted according to the expected input of the model.Here, we send an HTTP POST request to TorchServe, which is serving the **fishnet** model, and receive a prediction in response.

If everything is set up correctly, you should receive a prediction from the model, demonstrating that TorchServe is successfully running and handling inference requests.

Monitoring and Managing TorchServe

TorchServe also provides built-in monitoring and logging to help manage deployed models in production. You can view logs to check the status of the service and manage running models. By default, logs are stored in the **logs/** directory of your TorchServe installation.

You can also stop the TorchServe instance when it's no longer needed:

```
torchserve --stop
```

This setup allows the model to handle real-time requests, making it production-ready for deployment in real-world applications.

Deploying Models for Production

Once the trained neural network model is successfully packaged and served through **TorchServe**, the next crucial step is deploying it into a production environment. This involves addressing essential concerns like **multi-model serving**, **model versioning**, **monitoring**, and **logging**, all of which help ensure that the deployed model can handle real-world usage, remain scalable, and be easily updated. In this section, we will continue from where we left off in the previous topic, exploring these advanced features of TorchServe and how they apply to our neural network model trained on the **fish dataset**.

Multi-Model Serving with TorchServe

In production environments, it's often necessary to serve multiple models at the same time. For instance, a service might need to serve models for different tasks (e.g., image classification and object detection) or serve multiple versions of the same model for A/B testing or model comparison. TorchServe provides an efficient way to load, manage, and serve multiple models concurrently.

To set this up, follow these steps:

Packaging Second Model

Assume you have another PyTorch model trained on a similar dataset, perhaps called **FishNetV2**. First, package this model just as we did with the first one:

- Create a **model_v2.py** file defining the new architecture (which may be similar to **FishNet** or slightly modified).
- Archive the second model using the **torch-model-archiver** command, just as we did previously:

```
torch-model-archiver --model-name fishnetv2 --version 1.0 \
    --model-file model_v2.py --serialized-file fishnet_v2.pth \
    --handler torchserve/handlers/image_classifier \
```

```
    --export-path ./model-store --extra-files
index_to_name_v2.json
```

This will create a **fishnetv2.mar** file in the **model-store** directory.

Serving Multiple Models

To serve both models simultaneously, we need to tell TorchServe to load both **FishNet** and **FishNetV2** models when starting the server. We can do this by modifying the **--models** argument to include both models:

```
torchserve --start --model-store model-store --models
fishnet=fishnet.mar,fishnetv2=fishnetv2.mar
```

TorchServe will now serve both models under different names (**fishnet** and **fishnetv2**). Each model will have its own API endpoint for predictions.

Sending Requests to Different Models

When sending inference requests, you can specify which model to use by targeting its specific endpoint. Given below is an example of how to send a request to the **fishnetv2** model:

```
# Prepare the input for FishNetV2

input_data = [[0.3, 0.8, 1.0, 0.6, 0.7]]


# Send the request to the FishNetV2 model endpoint

response =
requests.post("http://127.0.0.1:8080/predictions/fishnetv
2", data=json.dumps({"data": input_data}))


# Print the prediction

print(response.json())
```

By sending requests to the specific model endpoint, you can manage multiple models within the same TorchServe instance without conflict. This allows for flexible deployment scenarios, such as hosting models for different tasks, running A/B tests between models, or using different models for different user groups.

Versioning Models with TorchServe

Model versioning in production ensures that updates to a model can be tested and deployed without interrupting the service. TorchServe makes it easy to deploy multiple versions of the same model.

We will see below how we can serve multiple versions of our **FishNet** model.

Versioning FishNet Model

Assume we have trained an updated version of **FishNet** (e.g., after collecting more data or fine-tuning the architecture). We can save this new version as **fishnet_v2.pth** and package it with an updated version number:

```
torch-model-archiver --model-name fishnet --version 2.0 \
   --model-file model.py --serialized-file fishnet_v2.pth
\
   --handler torchserve/handlers/image_classifier \
   --export-path ./model-store --extra-files
index_to_name.json
```

This command creates a new model archive (**fishnet.mar**) with version 2.0.

Serving Multiple Versions

To serve both versions (1.0 and 2.0) simultaneously, use the **--models** argument to specify the different versions:

```
torchserve --start --model-store model-store --models
fishnet=fishnet.mar
```

TorchServe automatically handles versioning behind the scenes. You can specify which version of the model to use for inference by adding a version parameter to the request:

- For version 1.0:

```
response =
requests.post("http://127.0.0.1:8080/predictions/fishnet?
version=1.0", data=json.dumps({"data": input_data}))
```

- For version 2.0:

```
response =
requests.post("http://127.0.0.1:8080/predictions/fishnet?
version=2.0", data=json.dumps({"data": input_data}))
```

By specifying the model version in the request, you can deploy and test new versions without disrupting the service provided by older versions.

Monitoring and Logging

Monitoring and logging are essential for keeping track of model performance, identifying bottlenecks, and troubleshooting errors in production. TorchServe comes with built-in support for both **metrics** and **logging**, allowing developers and engineers to monitor deployed models in real-time.

Accessing Logs in TorchServe

TorchServe generates logs that provide detailed information about requests, errors, model loading, and performance metrics. By default, logs are stored in the **logs/** directory of your TorchServe installation.

You can view the logs to monitor the server's activity:

```
tail -f logs/model_log.log
```

This log file captures events such as model load/unload operations, requests received, and responses sent. It's useful for troubleshooting issues like model failures or latency spikes.

Enabling and Viewing Metrics

TorchServe also provides real-time metrics, such as request throughput, model inference time, and errors. These metrics can be exposed to monitoring tools like **Prometheus** and visualized with **Grafana** for easy monitoring.

To enable metrics, modify the TorchServe configuration file (**config.properties**) to expose a metrics endpoint:

```
inference_address=http://127.0.0.1:8080

management_address=http://127.0.0.1:8081

metrics_address=http://127.0.0.1:8082

enable_metrics=true
```

Once metrics are enabled, you can access them through the **metrics_address** specified above:

```
curl http://127.0.0.1:8082/metrics
```

This command returns a list of metrics such as inference latency, total number of requests, and the number of failed requests.

Using Prometheus for Monitoring

To integrate with **Prometheus**, configure Prometheus to scrape the metrics from the TorchServe endpoint. Given below is an example configuration for **prometheus.yml**:

```
scrape_configs:

  - job_name: 'torchserve'

    metrics_path: '/metrics'

    static_configs:

      - targets: ['127.0.0.1:8082']
```

Once set up, Prometheus will start collecting metrics from TorchServe, which can be visualized using **Grafana** or other monitoring tools.

Scaling and Production Considerations

For large-scale production environments, models often need to be scaled to handle high traffic volumes. TorchServe supports scaling through its **multi-worker** architecture, where multiple instances of the same model can run concurrently to handle requests.

Configuring Model Workers

To scale a model, you can configure the number of workers (processes) assigned to the model in the **config.properties** file:

```
model_name=fishnet

number_of_workers=4
```

This configuration assigns four workers to the **FishNet** model, allowing it to handle more requests in parallel. Workers can also be dynamically scaled up or down based on traffic demands.

Handling High-Volume Requests

When deploying models in high-traffic production environments, it's crucial to ensure that the system can handle large volumes of requests without performance degradation. TorchServe's built-in support for **batch inference** allows you to group multiple inference requests into a single batch, improving throughput and reducing the overall time spent processing requests.

Batching can be configured per model by setting the **batch_size** and **max_batch_delay** parameters in the **config.properties** file:

```
batch_size=16

max_batch_delay=100
```

This configuration processes batches of up to 16 requests at once, with a maximum delay of 100 milliseconds before a batch is sent for inference.

In a production scenario where real-time model inference is required—such as classifying fish species from images, as in our project—TorchServe's ability to serve both the **FishNet** and **FishNetV2** models concurrently allows for testing new versions of the model (using A/B testing techniques) while ensuring that the live version continues to operate seamlessly. This enables us to update models incrementally without risking downtime or performance degradation, which is critical for applications requiring continuous, uninterrupted service.

With the multi-model setup, you could even deploy additional models trained for different tasks—like fish detection or anomaly detection in fish health—alongside the existing classification models. TorchServe makes it easy to manage these models through its REST API, with endpoints for each model and its respective versions.

Summary

In this chapter, the focus was on deploying PyTorch models into production environments using TorchServe. TorchServe, an open-source model serving framework, enabled the seamless deployment of trained neural network models by providing a scalable, production-ready system. One of the key areas learned was multi-model serving, which allowed for multiple models to be deployed concurrently, making it possible to handle different tasks or versions of the same model simultaneously. This capability proved useful in environments where both the original model and an updated version needed to be available for inference, such as the FishNet models from our project.

Another critical aspect explored was model versioning. By leveraging TorchServe's built-in versioning support, different iterations of a model could be deployed without disrupting the service. This made it easier to roll out new updates or test different versions of a model without risking performance issues or downtime. The chapter also covered the importance of monitoring and logging, essential for tracking the performance of models in real-time. TorchServe offered extensive logging and metrics tracking capabilities, which could be integrated with tools like Prometheus and Grafana for more detailed insights into model behavior and system performance.

Scaling models through multi-worker processes and handling high-volume requests with batching were other vital features learned, allowing the service to efficiently manage increased traffic while maintaining low latency. Overall, the chapter provided a comprehensive understanding of how TorchServe facilitates the deployment, monitoring, and management of PyTorch models in production, making it a robust solution for handling real-time inference and large-scale machine learning applications.

Index

R

T

U

W

Epilogue

As I conclude this second edition of Learning PyTorch 2.0, I am confident that I have delivered a valuable resource that will bring you immense satisfaction. I am proud to say that writing this book has been an intense but rewarding journey that reflects the incredible growth and evolution of PyTorch and its community. This edition demanded that I explore newer, more advanced topics while refining the core teachings from the first edition. I made it my mission to ensure that every chapter, every concept, and every hands-on example equips you with the practical skills you need to excel in deep learning and neural network development. When I first started revisiting the material for this edition, I knew I had more to share. PyTorch has introduced game-changing features like torch.compile(), which drastically improve model training and inference speeds. I was eager to bring these new capabilities into the book. I made sure the updates were meaningful changes that would make a real difference in how you work with PyTorch in production. Now that I've finished this book, I feel a great sense of relief. I've effectively passed on what I've learned about optimizing PyTorch to you.

I am delighted to say that a key benefit of writing this second edition has been to reinforce the practical, real-world focus of the book. I made a deliberate choice to use the fish dataset. I have always believed that you should not just work with artificial examples but apply what you learn to realistic problems. As you have moved through the chapters, whether building neural networks, deploying models with TorchServe, or migrating between frameworks, you have done so in a way that mirrors real development environments. I am confident that I have provided you with executable, ready-to-run programs. The expanded material on model deployment, multi-model serving, and versioning is particularly rewarding. These reflect the growing importance of scalable production deployments in modern machine learning. I knew these were areas that needed more attention, and I'm pleased that I was able to dive deeper into them this time. I am confident that you will use what you have learned here to build models, deploy them, and maintain them efficiently in real-world applications. Teaching this has been one of the highlights of my professional journey.

I am pleased to say that I have delivered everything I intended to in this book. I did not always enjoy the process of writing, revising, and expanding the content, but I am certain it was worth it. Each chapter was designed to help you become more confident in your PyTorch skills and in your ability to build and deploy neural networks. I am confident that by working through this book, you will share that same feeling of satisfaction. You've mastered the fundamentals of neural networks, tackled complex architectures, and learned how to optimize performance. I am certain that you have gained not only technical knowledge but also the confidence to apply it in your own projects. Thank you for joining me on this journey—it's been a great one.

Thank You

www.ingramcontent.com/pod-product-compliance
Lightning Source LLC
Chambersburg PA
CBHW080213170726
48282CB00030B/1102
* 9 7 8 8 1 1 9 1 7 7 9 1 2 *